TO YOUR NAME

A Study of the Psalms

Volume 1

by Hal Hammons

ONESTONE
BIBLICAL RESOURCES

Published by:
One Stone Press
979 Lovers Lane
Bowling Green, KY 42103

Printed in the United States of Americau

ISBN (10 Digit): 1-941422-17-9
ISBN (13 Digit): 978-1-941422-17-5

Supplemental Materials Available:
PowerPoint slides for each lesson
Answer key
Downloadable PDF

Table of Contents

To Your Name
An Introduction for the Reader

The Psalms have always fascinated me—their breadth of content, their Messianic implications, their evident importance in the lives of First Century Christians—the reasons abound. And that is not even accounting for their uplifting and encouraging nature. It is certainly the most read book in the Old Testament, and perhaps the most read in the Bible.

Studying Psalms can be problematical. There is the obvious problem of size. Spending quality time with 150 individual psalms would take years in a normal church Bible class; and as important as every aspect of God's word is, including the poetry, few would suggest topics such as the life of Christ and the behavior of the early church should be neglected for extended periods of time. Also, Psalms tends to be repetitive, as any collection of similarly themed poems this large inevitably will be. (Psalms 14 and 53 are almost identical!) We all like our Bible study to be somewhat practical; it can be challenging trying to relate to David in the wilderness or Judah returning from Babylon. Then, of course, are the imprecatory psalms—those that call down God's righteous wrath upon His enemies. (Killing babies? Really?) It can get uncomfortable even reading those, let alone seeing them as a reflection of the character of God. Often we simply choose to play "priest and Levite" with them—just pass by on the other side.

To Your Name is different from any other book I have seen. In it you will be taken on a tour of the Psalter (not an exhaustive one, but a comprehensive one). Each lesson will feature a single psalm, focusing on a particular audience and a particular message. The lesson will help you study the psalm in question in seven different ways:

- A brief look at the psalm itself.
- An insight into the use of figurative language as it is used in the psalm.
- A Bible lesson about a character who fits in the scope of the psalm.
- A secondary psalm to study in brief, helping to show the pattern of topic development throughout the Psalter.
- A "case study" of a person in the modern day that relates to the topic at hand.
- A look into the New Testament at a story, character or text that is brought into sharper relief by considering a verse or term from one of the two selected psalms.
- Finally, a modern-day hymn relating to the topic, and a discussion of how we can use hymns of this nature to emphasize points being taught in the psalm.

This is a lot of studying to do. It was written with the idea that a group could spend two 45-minute sessions on each lesson. The teacher notes included here will follow that plan. However, individual teachers and classes are encouraged to proceed at their own pace, whether faster or slower.

The Bible class to which I allude in the "A Worship Study" section is fictitious. The people referenced therein, as well as the "case studies," are also fictitious. Similarities to actual persons are not intended and should not be inferred.

To facilitate the use of this book in an actual Bible study centered around hymns, and for the reader's personal growth in song worship, I include a section at the end of each lesson where readers are encouraged to come up with hymns that address the same general theme. Some hymns are more acceptable for public worship than others; different Christians will have different standards. The purpose is to encourage us to choose not only "scriptural" songs for worship but also the ones that are most appropriate. Thoughtfulness is always important for the readers to employ in worship; there is always room for improvement there.

I include in the teacher's notes a public reading of the primary psalm. I strongly encourage you to make time for that. The full psalm is included in the material for that purpose. The full psalm quotations, and all other Scripture references unless otherwise indicated, are from the Holman Christian Standard Bible, which I found very effective in balancing easy and emotional reading with accurate content. The public reading of Scripture is an art that, in my judgment, has been allowed to deteriorate horribly. An effective reading of the text is more effective in retaining the group's attention, focusing on the content, and deriving the appropriate message. Either the moderator or (even better) a single volunteer from the audience is encouraged to read the text from the book, with everyone else following along. I think you will find the exercise well worth the small amount of time it takes. (It is "Bible study" after all.)

The material encourages the reader to read the psalm multiple times. The teacher should not feel compelled to have a public recitation every time I write, "Read Psalm X again"; that note is more for the student than for the class. But please try to read it aloud at the beginning of the lesson — and if time permits, again at the end.

If I left your own personal favorite psalm out, I apologize. I only hope this study will encourage you to develop a new favorite, or several.

Tim Berman gets the credit for typesetting the hymns in the book. It says all you need to know about Tim that he wanted to be paid for his work in hymnals. That is the mark of a man who loves to sing praises and to assist others in doing so. May his tribe increase.

A special word of thanks goes out to the estate of A.W. Dicus for granting permission for the use of "Our God, He is Alive"—the hymn that has been often referred to as the unofficial "national anthem" of churches of Christ, and is in one writer's opinion perhaps the greatest hymn of the 20th Century. Our usage of the hymn is limited and specific. Unauthorized usage of copyrighted material is theft; theft is a sin. If you want to make copies of this or any other protected hymn, please get permission through the proper channels.

And to Bro. Dicus and the other tremendously talented men and women who give us songs to sing, so many of them departed now—simply saying "Thank you" seems horribly inadequate. But, "Thank you" all the same.

Finally, my brethren:
Not to us LORD, not to us, but to Your name give glory
because of Your faithful love, because of Your truth, (Psalm 115:1).

Hal Hammons
Pace, Florida
June 2015

Teachers Notes

The following is a suggested plan for a class schedule using *To Your Name*, assuming two 45-minute class periods per lesson:

Class 1:

- Read the primary psalm aloud from the book. (5 minutes)
- Discuss the psalm and answer the questions. (20 minutes)
- Discuss figures of speech, including the one highlighted. (5 minutes)
- Discuss the "Bible Study" section and answer the questions. (15 minutes)
- Read the primary psalm aloud again if time permits.

Class 2:

- Discuss the secondary psalm; read it aloud from the text of the reader's choosing if it is not too long. (15 minutes)
- Discuss the "Case Study" section, and answer the questions. (10 minutes)
- Discuss the "New Testament Insight" section. (10 minutes)
- Discuss the "Hymn Study" and "Worship Study" sections, and discuss students' answers to the "Worship Study" question. Sing the song as a group if you wish. (10 minutes)
- If time permits, discuss other appropriate or inappropriate hymns along the same theme.

To Mom, who taught me to sing;
To Bert Dodd, who taught me to sing correctly;
And to Jesse Jenkins, who taught me why to sing.

Psalm 1
A Song for the Student

When most people think of being "happy," they think of situations—love, money, success in business, etc. But the Biblical idea of happiness or blessedness goes far deeper. In passages such as the Beatitudes (Matthew 5:3-12), the "blessed" life is described as one in which blessings can be found. Those blessings typically are more spiritual than physical. God, who created human beings, can obviously be expected to know what is the best life for a human being. The Bible describes that life.

It comes as no surprise, then, that God's "happy" life is not found by going where people frequently go; and it certainly is not found where wicked people go. Their idea of happiness could not be further from God's. Wicked people will go toward places where their wicked lusts will be gratified. And sin, like misery, loves company. So they will delight in trying to indoctrinate righteous souls in the ways of the devil.

The progressive nature of sin's influence has been frequently pointed out from Psalm 1:1. First one listens to poor advice; then he goes in poor directions; then, before long, he has officially joined company with people who make no effort to hide their disdain for God's approved lifestyle.

The alternative found by the righteous one is found in pursuit of God's ways through His holy word. He delights in it, and he spends quality time throughout his day and week in pursuit of its application. It is not enough for him to have simply found a better way; he wants to grow in that way and walk more

¹ How happy is the man
who does not follow the advice
   of the wicked,
or take the path of sinners,
or join a group of mockers!
² Instead, his delight is in the
   LORD's instruction,
and he meditates on it day and
   night.
³ He is like a tree planted beside
   streams of water
that bears its fruit in season
and whose leaf does not wither.
Whatever he does prospers.
⁴ The wicked are not like this;
instead, they are like chaff that
   the wind blows away.
⁵ Therefore the wicked will not
   survive the judgment,
and sinners will not be in the
   community of the righteous.
⁶ For the LORD watches over the
   way of the righteous,
but the way of the wicked leads
   to ruin.

perfectly in it. As a result, he is "like a tree planted beside streams of water that bears its fruit in season and whose leaf does not wither." He has the stability he needs not only to survive in a hostile world, but also to produce utility and beauty in it.

The wicked, on the other hand, is the opposite. He is as firmly rooted as sawdust, and the winds of God's judgment will carry him away. His destruction may not come in the immediate term, of course, but the firmly rooted student of God's word will be there to see it when it happens—if not in this life, then certainly in the next.

1. What are some obvious signs that we are trying to be students of God's word? What are some obvious signs that we are not? _____

   _____

   _____

   _____

2. At what point is a "sinner" to be cut out of "the community of the righteous" in the modern day? Cite Scripture, and describe briefly how it might be done.

   _____

   _____

   _____

3. In what way does the righteous "prosper" when he delights in God's instruc-tion? Is there any way that he might not "prosper"? Explain. _____

   _____

   _____

   _____

4. What is your favorite line in the psalm? Why? _____

   _____

   _____

   _____

The Student: A Bible Study

Apollos knew a great bit of the truth already. He knew about the Law of Moses. He knew about the promise of the Messiah. He knew about Jesus Himself. Being a disciple of John the Baptist, one can safely assume he knew about confessing his sins (Matthew 3:6), the necessity of true repentance (Matthew 3:8), and the role of repentance and baptism in the removal of sins (Mark 1:4). This is more than a great many "disciples" acknowledge even today.

However, he did not fully understand about baptism in the name of Jesus, as was practiced by the apostles on the day of Pentecost (Acts 2:38); rather, "he

---

A Planted Tree

Figure of Speech

A tree symbolizes stability. It may sway with the wind, but it remains in place because it is solidly structured above ground and firmly rooted below the surface. The deeper and more far-reaching the root structure, the easier it is for the tree to find the life-sustaining water in times of hardship. Of course, being "planted beside streams of water" helps tremendously.

The tree must serve its desired purpose, though. In Luke 13:6-9, Jesus tells a parable in which a land owner despairs of ever finding fruit on his fig tree—fruit being the reason he planted the tree in the first place. We can be confident that, nourished by God's word and freshened by the water Jesus provides (John 4:14), we will remain spiritually healthy and produce much fruit in His name.

---

knew only John's baptism" (Acts 18:25). This seems to indicate he was baptizing people in the same way he was, presumably, baptized by John. And by "the same way," we do not mean immersion; no one was baptized in any way other than immersion in the New Testament, as that is what the Greek word for baptism literally means. No, it likely means something as seemingly insignificant as failing to acknowledge Jesus as Lord and as the true source of forgiveness.

What may seem like a technicality to us was significant to Aquila and Priscilla, who heard Apollos preach in Ephesus and were moved to explain "the way of God to him more accurately" (Acts 18:26). And given the further fellowship between Apollos and the two, and between his work and Paul's in Corinth later (1 Corinthians 3:6), it was not a "technicality" to Apollos, either. Being devoted to God, and to his quest for the truth, kept him from bristling or becoming defensive when his understanding was questioned. The same devotion to the Scriptures he demonstrated in his partial ignorance moved him to learn a better, more perfect way, and to go his way serving his God even more completely than he did before.

Apollos is cited in 1 Corinthians 3 as having a profound impact for good on the church in Corinth; certainly Paul gives no indication he blames Apollos at all for the faction that had developed in the church around his teaching. Years later, after Paul's first imprisonment, Apollos was still traveling throughout this part of the world preaching the gospel; we know because Paul wrote to encourage his protégé Titus to help Apollos and his fellow traveler, Zenas the lawyer, when they came through Crete (Titus 3:13).

Read Psalm 1 again—this time with Apollos in mind.

1. Cite Scriptures describing the proper attitude of one being corrected in a matter of doctrine or behavior, and the proper attitude of one doing the correcting. _____

   _____

   _____

   _____

2. Find another Biblical example, good or bad, of a student. Describe his or her inter-action with God's word. _____

   _____

   _____

   _____

Psalm 119—A Parallel Study

The longest psalm is also, for many, the one with the most familiar verses. Over and over again, in virtually every one of its 176 verses, the psalmist extols the virtues of the word of God. It keeps the young pure (v. 9). It gives life (v. 25). It gives hope (v. 49). It gives comfort (v. 52). It gives wisdom (v. 98). It gives guidance (v. 105). On and on we could go.

The first verse—"How happy are those whose way is blameless, who live according to the law of the LORD"—echoes the sentiment of the first verse of the entire Psalter and sets the tone for the wisdom of the next 175 verses. (It is ironic that the longest chapter in the Bible should begin so similarly as the longest book.) The truly blessed life is the one spent pursuing God's will instead of one's own will.

1. Read Psalm 119 thoroughly. Find a verse whose teachings you have difficulty putting into practice and explain why. _____

   _____

   _____

   _____

2. Describe a circumstance from your life of which you were reminded while reading the psalm. _____

   _____

   _____

3. How much time is appropriate to spend in a study of God's word? Explain.

   _____

   _____

   _____

4. What is your favorite line in the psalm? Why? _____

_____

_____

_____

The Student: A Case Study

Case File

AMBER
- 17 years old
- High school student
- Having trouble with friends who have worldly values

Until her junior year of high school, Amber was never in any trouble. She managed to avoid all the high school drinking parties, she refused the joint offered to her in the stands at the football game one night, and she was regular in her attendance at worship services and church functions. A big part of that was her friend, Josie, who (although not a Christian in the fullest sense) shared most of the same values.

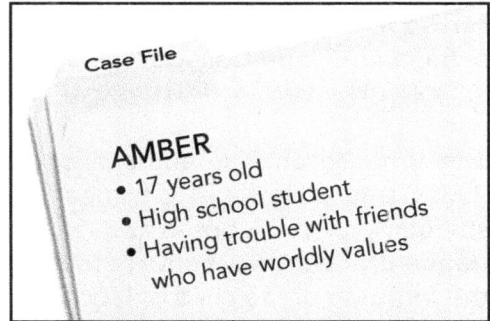

This changed when Josie got a boyfriend, Nate, who loved to party. Suddenly Amber was getting pressure to join in with all the activities she had easily avoided in times past. She did not want to lose a friend she had treasured for years. Then again, she knew her parents would not approve of the changes she was seeing in Josie, and they might even try to separate the two of them.

One Friday Josie picked Amber up for what was supposed to be a "girls' night out" but turned out to be a double-date, pairing Amber with Nate's friend, Ronnie. Amber had a crush on Ronnie in middle school, but his partying ways had become, if anything, even more rowdy than Nate's. Surprise, surprise.

Amber was in tears as her father picked her up close to midnight in a seedy-looking diner across the street from the nightclub where the party had wound up. "Thanks for calling," he said as they walked to the car. "I'm very proud of you." Unable to speak, Amber just nodded. They rode in silence all the way home.

Read Psalm 1—this time with Amber in mind.

What would you say to Amber based on Psalm 1? _____

_____

_____

_____

The Student: A Hymn Study

Psalm 1 provides the inspiration for "I Shall Not Be Moved," a hymn with deep roots in the African-American community. Edward Boatner is credited with the song in its current form, although it dates back much further and the lyrics vary widely between publications. A professional musician and singer, Boatner served as music director of the National Baptist Convention and as a professor at Samuel Huston College (now Huston-Tillotson University) and Wiley College in Texas. He died in 1981.

The song became an anthem for the American labor movement in the early 20th Century. However, it gained far more life when as was the case with many spirituals, it was co-opted as a rallying cry by the civil rights movement. Crowds frequently changed the lyrics to "We shall not be, we shall not be moved," as the fortitude of the child of God under assault in an ungodly world was seen as inspiration to African-Americans who felt oppressed during the turmoil of the 1960s.

Maya Angelou, the famous African-American poet, entitled one of her books of poetry *I Shall Not Be Moved* in reference to the hymn.

"I Shall Not Be Moved" is a favorite among country music aficionados and has been recorded frequently, perhaps most famously by the "Million Dollar Quartet" of Elvis Presley, Johnny Cash, Jerry Lee Lewis and Carl Perkins. Cash also included it on his own album produced late in his life, *My Mother's Hymn Book*. Charley Patton, one of the pioneers in the blues music of the American South, made perhaps the first recording of the song in 1929.

The Student: A Worship Study

Since our study in the Psalms started with Psalm 1, and since "I Shall Not Be Moved" is clearly based in Psalm 1, that seemed like the obvious song to pair with the first lesson. As I do with many songs that have choruses that basically repeat the music from the verse ("I am Bound for the Promised Land," "Tell Me the Story of Jesus," etc.), I asked that we sing the chorus only once. That made for a spirited rendition of the old classic, a song that, frankly, I had never cared for that much. My perception of "I Shall Not Be Moved" changed considerably that night.

"The plan is to ask the group what the song means to each of you, especially in the context of Psalm 1 and the context of your own life. Anyone want to go first?" I had no idea what sort of a hornet's nest I had stirred up.

"I remember my dad singing this song any time a stump we were trying to dig out was especially stubborn. *I shall not be, I shall not be moved...*"

I Shall Not Be Moved

1. Glo - ry hal - le - lu - jah, I shall not be moved;
2. In His love a - bid-ing, I shall not be moved;
3. Though all hell as - sail me, I shall not be moved;
4. Though the tem-pest rag - es, I shall not be moved,

An - chored in Je - ho - vah, I shall not be moved;
And in Him con - fid - ing, I shall not be moved;
Je - sus will not fail me, I shall not be moved;
On the Rock of Ag - es, I shall not be moved;

Fine

Just like a tree that's plant - ed by the wa - ters, I shall not be moved.

REFRAIN

D.S. al Fine

I shall not be, I shall not be moved, I shall not be, I shall not be moved,
I shall not be moved,

Words: Edward H. Boatner
Music: American Folk Melody

G - 4 - DO

"My grandmother sang this song from her bed any time one of her children talked about putting her in a nursing home. *I shall not be, I shall not be moved...*"

"I whisper it to myself whenever I watch Frozen with my kids and I don't want to start crying. *I shall not be, I shall not be moved...*"

Then Allen spoke up, and it got a bit more serious. "My grandfather told the story of how he invited some brethren from the church across town to a gospel meeting. The *black* church, I mean. Some good ol' boys burned the church building down that night."

"What did they do?" I asked, astonished.

"They met again the next night, outside on the church grounds, with lanterns for light. With the black brethren. '*I shall not be, I shall not be moved...*'"

What does "I Shall Not Be Moved" mean to you? _____
_____
_____
_____

The Bible Study Song List

If you were putting a list together for a study about Bible study, what songs would you include? Why? _____
_____
_____

What songs might you exclude? Why? _____
_____
_____

Psalm 2
A Song for the Messiah

When you think about it, it's really kind of funny—the nations of the world united against one Man. Schemes are concocted. Wars are waged. Conspiracies are formed. Such has been the case since long before Jesus walked in Galilee; such will be the case as long as the world stands. It is true whether you consider the planning to be figurative—sinful man working against the interests of a righteous Savior—or the literal machinations of governments, societies and influential individuals dragging the cause of Christ through the mud.

Mankind is determined to reject the authority of Jesus Christ which He received from His Father (Matthew 28:18). Mankind considers His requirements akin to slavery—which it is, after a fashion (Romans 6:17-18). And mankind is convinced it can win its protracted, millennia-long effort to be its own master, its own god—that it owes no allegiance whatsoever to its Creator or to His Son who came to deliver mankind from the sins it denies it committed or that even exist.

No wonder God laughs.

Do not take God's reaction to rebellion as being in any way indifferent. Jesus Himself told several parables illustrating the wrath from heaven

[1] Why do the nations rebel
and the peoples plot in vain?
[2] The kings of the earth take their stand
and the rulers conspire together
against the LORD and His Anointed One:
[3] "Let us tear off their chains
and free ourselves from their restraints."
[4] The One enthroned in heaven laughs;
the LORD ridicules them.
[5] Then He speaks to them in His anger
and terrifies them in His wrath:
[6] "I have consecrated My King
on Zion, My holy mountain."
[7] I will declare the LORD's decree:
He said to Me, "You are My Son;
today I have become Your Father.
[8] Ask of Me,
and I will make the nations Your inheritance
and the ends of the earth Your possession.
[9] You will break them with a rod of iron;
You will shatter them like pottery.
[10] So now, kings, be wise;
receive instruction, you judges of the earth.
[11] Serve the LORD with reverential awe,
and rejoice with trembling.
[12] Pay homage to the Son, or He will be angry
and you will perish in your rebellion,
for His anger may ignite at any moment.
All those who take refuge in Him are happy.

against those who would refuse to give His Son the proper consideration (Luke 13:6-9; 20:9-18; etc.).

God became the Father of Jesus in a way unlike any other of His sons. He literally "begot" Him in the womb of Mary. But also He named Him the proper recipient of the inheritance He was to bestow. Hebrews 11:17 records how Isaac became Abraham's "unique" son (the King James Version reads "only begotten son") when he was named the recipient of the spiritual blessing that God gave Abraham and that was passed along for generations leading up to Jesus Himself. Likewise, God's relationship with His other children, however special, does not in any way measure up to the one He has with this Son. Yes, as God's children, we are glorified and sanctified by the Father like Jesus is (Hebrews 2:10-11), but "the firstborn among many brothers" (Romans 8:29) does not share a plane of authority with us by any means. We owe Him the same honor we owe the Father; we reject the Father when we reject Him.

1. In what ways specifically can one see sinful mankind "conspire against the LORD and His Anointed One"? _____

_____

_____

_____

2. Find New Testament passages that quote Psalm 2:7. What point about Jesus and His authority are made there? _____

_____

_____

_____

3. In what sense is mere refusal to worship tantamount to rebellion? _____

_____

_____

_____

4. What is your favorite line in the psalm? Why? _____

_____

_____

_____

The Messiah: A Bible Study

The return of prophecy to Israel in persons such as Simeon and Anna (Luke 2:25-38), the appearances of angels (Matthew 1:20; Luke 1:11, 26-27), and the rise of the fourth world empire, Rome (Daniel 2:41-44), all indicated to the Jews that the time of the Messiah was upon them. But the greatest sign of all was the

---

Pay Homage   **Figure of Speech**

The notion of worship is as complex as you want it to be. At its root, acknowledging God is a simple act of will—admitting He rules and not we ourselves. In full flower, however, to the fervent and informed believer, worship is an act, or a series of acts, that connote not just a doctrinal and submissive connection to God, but an emotional one as well.

"Kiss the Son," reads the first phrase in Psalm 2:12 in many versions, including the English Standard and the New King James. This is not a kiss of fellowship, as in Genesis 33:4 and Romans 16:16. This is the kiss of worship, an acknowledgement of the innate superiority and worthiness of another, whether it is to Baal (1 Kings 19:18), created things (Job 31:27), or as is the case here—a demonstration of devotion to the Son. Just as Samuel subjected himself to the king he himself had just anointed (1 Samuel 10:1), so also we pay homage to the One whom the Heavenly Father has anointed as our King. Let us do it out of reverence, appreciation and love—but if we cannot manage that, at least let us do it out of fear of His wrath.

---

ministry of Jesus' cousin, John. In Matthew 11:14, Jesus attaches John to the fulfillment of the prophecy of the coming of Elijah in Malachi 4:5.

The prophecies regarding both Elijah and the Messiah were confusing to many in that day. Some equated the two. Some thought the Messiah was going to be just another prophet, perhaps a bit greater in some way than the others (Matthew 16:14). Herod Antipas, who had John thrown in prison and eventually beheaded, was moved by guilt to suggest Jesus was John himself raised from the dead (Matthew 14:1-2).

John's preaching left no question as to what he thought on the matter. He "came baptizing in the wilderness and preaching a baptism of repentance for the forgiveness of sins" (Mark 1:4). But his preaching did not emphasize himself or his own doctrine, rather the One who was yet to come.

By preaching repentance, he let t be known in no uncertain terms that the people of God, the literal descendants of Abraham, were not fit to receive the King who was to come. He said, as recorded in Matthew 3:8-9, "And don't presume to say to yourselves, 'We have Abraham as our father.' For I tell you that God is able to raise up children for Abraham from these stones!" In the next verse, he warned them that those found unworthy would be "cut down and thrown into the fire."

Repentance could not remain merely conceptual; John required "fruit consistent with repentance" (Matthew 3:8) from those who claimed to be interested in his gospel. From those who came to him for spiritual guidance, he required kindness toward others above and beyond the strict interpretation of the law, fair business practices, and contentment and honesty while dealing with those under your authority (Luke 3:10-14).

Through it all, John always emphasized the primacy of the One to come. John said Christ's baptism and his judgment would be far greater (Matthew 3:11-12). And when Jesus finally began His ministry, he reacted in words that could not be misunderstood: "You yourselves can testify that I said, 'I am not the Messiah, but I've been sent ahead of Him.... He must increase but I must decrease" (John 3:28-30).

Matthew, Mark and Luke quote Isaiah 40:3 and apply it to John saying it was he who was "a voice of one crying out in the wilderness: 'Prepare the way for the Lord; make His paths straight!'" And as Jesus pointed out to his detractors, those who failed to recognize John's message from on high were likely going to find an excuse to reject Jesus' teachings as well (Matthew 11:18-19).

Read Psalm 2 again—this time with John in mind.

1. Explain the gesture of service involved in the removal of another's sandals (Matthew 3:11) and what it says about John that he considered himself unworthy of it. Cite other Scriptures. _____
   _____
   _____
   _____

2. Read what John said about Jesus in John 1:29-34. What particulars about Jesus and his mission did John know, and how did he know it? _____
   _____
   _____
   _____

Psalm 110—A Parallel Study

The simple truth of Messiah's supremacy and authority prophesied in Psalm 110 confounded the Jews of Jesus' day. They were used to thinking of the Messiah as being a king roughly on a par with David, the one who established the nation and made it prominent on the world stage. But as Jesus points out (Matthew 22:44, Mark 12:36, Luke 20:42-24), the prophecy has David calling Him "my Lord." Clearly the inspired text identifies the Messiah as being superior to David, superior to everyone.

The exaltation of Jesus according to prophecy is one of the keystones of Peter's sermon on Pentecost. The combination of resurrection and coronation made it imperative that they accept guilt for the crucifixion and accept Jesus as the Messiah and Savior. The fate of those who refuse to submit, as indicated in the psalm, is too awful to contemplate.

1. Psalm 110:1 is referenced at least two other times in the New Testament. Find them and explain the application. _____

   _____

   _____

   _____

2. At what point do (or did) Jesus' enemies become His footstool? Do they become such voluntarily or involuntarily? _____

   _____

   _____

   _____

3. What kind of warfare is depicted in verses 5-6? Do you think this is talking about final judgment, or the success of His kingdom, or literal military conflict? Explain. _____

   _____

   _____

   _____

4. What is your favorite line in the psalm? Why? _____

   _____

   _____

   _____

The Messiah: A Case Study

Janet's study group for her philosophy class liked to deal with abstract concepts. Janet liked the mental exercise but loved having the constant of her faith to fall back on and give her stability in an increasingly unstable world. One day the subject of "proving" the Bible came up. Janet rose to the challenge, admitting the concept of faith did not depend ultimately upon evidence, but asserting that enough evidence was available for the fundamental issues to at least give some credibility to the Bible.

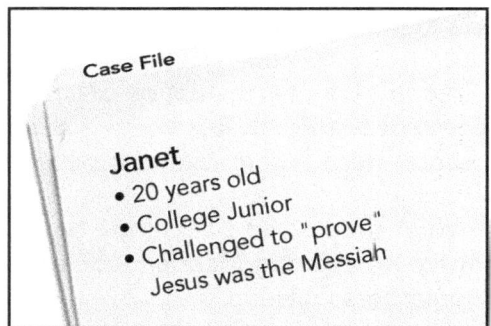

Case File

Janet
- 20 years old
- College Junior
- Challenged to "prove" Jesus was the Messiah

"Messianic prophecies, for instance," she said. "There are dozens of prophecies that Jesus fulfilled. That couldn't be an accident."

"But it could be staged," one agnostic friend suggested. "Or faked, or manipulated, or just plain made up."

"Not all of them, though," Janet insisted. "Not by a long shot." She committed to come back the next week with a list.

Instead she brought two. "The first is a list of prophecies Jesus could not possibly have fulfilled on purpose—that is, unless He was the Son of God. They were accomplished through forces either prior to His birth or completely separate from His own choices.

"In Genesis 49:10, He was said to be coming through the tribe of Judah. He did.

"In 2 Samuel 7:13, the throne of David is assured forever. Jesus claimed that throne as his descendant. Matthew 1 emphasizes the genealogy of Jesus and shows He was born to the right family.

"Daniel 2 describes four world kingdoms, fitting the world timeline of the Babylonian, Persian, Macedonian and Roman empires. Verse 44 says it would be during the days of those kings that God would establish His kingdom. Jesus was born in the days of the Roman Empire.

"Isaiah 7:14 said He would be born of a virgin. Even if you take the position (and I don't) that the Hebrew word for virgin denotes only a young woman, it still puts limitations on His mother. Luke 1:27 describes Mary as being an unmarried, childless and (one would have to assume) young woman.

"Micah 5:2 predicted He would be born in Bethlehem. Advisors to Herod the Great knew the prophecy and in Matthew 2:4-6 gave it Messianic application.

"Hosea 11:1 uses the nation of Israel as a type of the Messiah, saying He would come out of Egypt just like the nation did. Jesus' family took Him to Egypt to escape Herod's threats and brought Him back, according to Matthew 2:14-15.

"When they came back, they based themselves in Galilee, not in Jerusalem where an aspiring Messiah would want to be. Isaiah 9:1-2 prophesied that he would be a Galilean.

"Isaiah 40:6-9 describes a forerunner going before Him to prepare the way. John the Baptist fulfilled that before Jesus ever identified Himself as the Messiah."

"But all that would have been done just by being in the right place at the right time," said Janet's critic. "Dozens of people likely 'fulfilled' those prophecies just as much as Jesus did."

"That's where the second list comes in. Isaiah 35:5-6 says He would perform miracles. Malachi 3:1 says He would enter the temple. Zechariah 9:9 mentions Him entering triumphantly on the foal of a donkey. He did all those things."

"Well, people thought he did miracles, maybe. But anyone can ride a donkey."

"Well, you can't have it both ways." Janet said, chuckling. "It can't be a coincidence and a put-up job. The fact that such a variety of support for His Messianic claim is available—including things like the fulfillment of Isaiah 60:3 that His message would extend to the Gentiles, a prophecy fulfilled even after He had already left the earth—ought to at least open your mind up to consider the possibility."

"Well," said her opponent, arms crossed, "I'm not convinced."

"Well," said Janet smiling, "That's a fulfillment of prophecy, too. Isaiah 53:1— 'Who has believed what we have heard?'"

Read Psalm 2 again—this time with Janet in mind.

What would you say to Janet, based on Psalm 2? _____
_____
_____
_____

New Testament Insight

The LORD has sworn an oath and will not take it back:
"Forever, You are a priest like Melchizedek." — Psalm 110:4

It is said of Melchizedek in Hebrews 7:3 that he was "without father, mother, or genealogy, having neither beginning of days nor end of life, but resembling the Son of God." This is perhaps the clearest example in the Bible of type/antitype symbolism—the type, or foretaste, being the literal king and priest of ancient Salem; the antitype being the One who received his priesthood.

The point of Hebrews 7 is that there is Bible precedent for a priest of God not of Levi, and also a priest serving as king. Such was not permissible under the Law of Moses, the writer argues, and yet Psalm 110 clearly indicates that such would be the case for Messiah. Therefore, by necessary extension, the Law of Moses would have to be put aside for Messiah to reign and minister for us.

There is little doubt that "without father, mother or genealogy" in the case of Melchizedek is figurative; all humans have parents. The point is that Melchizedek appears from nowhere in the text and returns to nowhere after his work is done. He does not inherit or pass along his role. In the same way, Jesus does not require a pedigree, from Aaron or anyone else, or leave one; "Therefore He is always able to save those who come to God through Him, since He always lives to intercede for them" (Hebrews 7:25).

The Messiah: A Hymn Study

"Joy to the World" is not a Christmas carol.

At least, it was not written for that purpose. And when you think about it, it doesn't have any of the hallmarks of the traditional religious-themed carols. It never mentions shepherds or wise men. It never mentions Mary or Joseph. It does not even mention the birth of Christ. This is because Isaac Watts had a very different message in mind when he penned these words almost 300 years ago. He meant simply to glorify Jesus as the King who would usher in the age of the kingdom of prophecy; "He comes to make His blessings flow far as the curse is found."

Isaac Watts is called "the Father of Hymns" for a reason. Before Watts, hymn singing (at least, in England) consisted mostly of simply putting the Psalms to music, generally resulting in awkward phraseology and lethargic praise. Watts was the first to take the Psalms and rework them to accommodate New Testament teachings. His most famous example of this is "Joy to the World," which was based on Psalm 98:4-9. Instead of simply singing praises to God, instead we find ourselves praising the Son who came to reign as King of kings.

Dozens of the roughly 800 hymns Watts composed are still in common usage, among which are "When I Survey the Wondrous Cross," "I'm Not Ashamed to Own My Lord," "Am I a Soldier of the Cross?," "How Shall the Young Secure Their Hearts," and "Alas, and Did My Savior Bleed."

Lowell Mason, one of the most prolific and successful hymn composers of all time, is believed to have adapted a tune from George Fredric Handel, the composer of *The Messiah*, for "Joy to the World" in 1832.

The Messiah: A Worship Study

"I think it's a shame that we have pretty much surrendered our right to sing religious Christmas carols," Jake said after we sang "Joy to the World." Imme-

Joy to the World

1. Joy to the world, the Lord is come! Let earth re - ceive her King;
2. Joy to the earth, the Sav - ior reigns! Let men their songs em - ploy;
3. No more let sins and sor - rows grow, Nor thorns in - fest the ground;
4. He rules the world with truth and grace, And makes the na - tions prove

Let eve - ry heart pre - pare Him room,
While fields and floods, rocks, hills and plains
He comes to make His bless - ings flow
The glo - ries of His right - eous - ness,

And heav'n and na - ture sing, And heav'n and na - ture sing,
Re - peat the sound-ing joy, Re - peat the sound-ing joy,
Far as the curse is found, Far as the curse is found,
And won-ders of His love, And won-ders of His love,

1. And heav'n and na-ture sing.

And heav'n and na-

And heav'n, and heav'n, and na - ture sing.
Re - peat, re - peat, the sound-ing joy.
Far as, far as, the curse is found.
And won-ders, and won - ders, of His love.

ture sing.

Words: Isaac Watts
Music: Lowell Mason

D - 2 - DO

diately there arose a chorus of "Amens" the like of which I had certainly never heard during one of my sermons.

Jake continued, "I mean, I have heard all my life that Jesus was almost certainly not born on December 25, that our Christmas celebration is pagan in its origins, that the New Testament doesn't authorize celebrating Jesus' birth, that the early church didn't do it. And I agree with all that. Still, it has always struck me odd that we get upset about one of the few occasions in the year when our nation actually starts expressing an interest, however shallow or uninformed, in Jesus Christ."
"Exactly," I added. "So when is it OK to sing 'Joy to the World'? We feel weird singing it outside of the Christmas season. But we feel like we're compromising truth when we sing it during the Christmas season. And it's a shame, because it's a great song."

"Lots of so-called carols are. 'Silent Night, 'O Little Town of Bethlehem,' and 'Hark, the Herald Angels Sing' are all favorites of mine."

"You have to be careful with some," I cautioned. "'Away in a Manger' implies Jesus did not cry as an infant, which is an old superstition with no basis in Scripture. 'O Holy Night' puts the wise men at the manger scene, and Matthew's account says Jesus was in a house when they visited. And of course, there are the non-kings, of which they may or may not have been three. But I could hear 'Angels from the Realms of Glory,' 'O Come All Ye Faithful' or 'Mary, Did You Know?' every week of the year and not get tired of them."

"Maybe the answer," Jake suggested, "is just to take the songs for what they actually say, not what they mean in our society. If 'Joy to the World' is a Scriptural and profitable song, let's sing it and sing it often. The more we sing it in April and August, the less weird it will seem—and the better we will able to put it in its proper context when we hear it in December."

What does "Joy to the World" mean to you? _____
_____
_____
_____

The Bible Study Song List

If you were putting a list together for a study about the Messiah, what songs would you include? Why? _____
_____
_____

What songs might you exclude? Why? _____
_____
_____

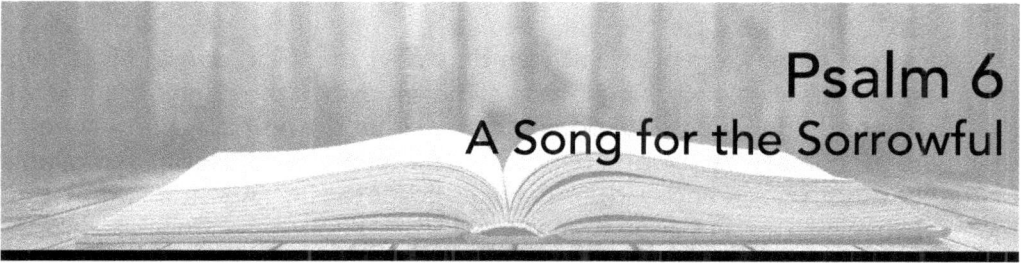

Psalm 6
A Song for the Sorrowful

A man is pining away for his late father. He misses him terribly. But worse than that, he blames himself. The stress he placed on his father almost certainly made his condition worse and hastened his death.

A woman misses her husband. Yes, he abandoned her. But she knows in her heart she was not the wife he needed. If she had behaved better, her marriage would still be alive and thriving.

A criminal is paying the due penalty for his crime. His future is dark, and his present is worse. He truly regrets his actions. But how many times must he be brought to repentance?

A child is at home crying while his younger brother is in the hospital. They both knew without even being told that they should not have been on the roof of their two-story house. But he had wanted to look like the big brother, capable of anything. And naturally, little brother wanted to be like big brother.

Each of them is thinking this may be God's way of teaching them a lesson. Perhaps even some cruel "friends," like Job's, have told them as much, and in their proclaimed efforts to help have made the situation far worse.

Well, lesson learned. Each has been brought to a level of repentance he or she had never known before. Surely it is time, then, for God to send relief to the broken spirits. But relief does not come. The feelings of guilt, hurt, frustration and pain continue and even worsen.

¹ LORD, do not rebuke me in Your anger;
do not discipline me in Your wrath.
² Be gracious to me, LORD, for I am weak;
heal me, LORD, for my bones are shaking;
³ my whole being is shaken with terror.
And You, LORD—how long?
⁴ Turn, LORD! Rescue me;
save me because of Your faithful love.
⁵ For there is no remembrance of You in death;
who can thank You in Sheol?
⁶ I am weary from my groaning;
with my tears I dampen my pillow
and drench my bed every night.
⁷ My eyes are swollen from grief;
they grow old because of all my enemies.
⁸ Depart from me, all evildoers,
for the LORD has heard the sound of my weeping.
⁹ The LORD has heard my plea for help;
the LORD accepts my prayer.
¹⁰ All my enemies will be ashamed and shake with terror;
they will turn back and suddenly be disgraced.

The person of faith is reminded in these dark days that God does, in fact, love His people. He is always working for their welfare, even if they don't see it at the time (Romans 8:28). Surely Paul does not mean that the horrible, hurtful events of life are in themselves "good" things. No, he means God uses all the events in our lives, both good and bad, to draw us closer to Him. And it could be that there is a level of trust and dependence that can only be reached in times of pain.

Psalm 6 is one of several psalms in which the subject spends much of the psalm giving air to his complaints, only to turn in the last verses and affirm his faith in a loving Lord. The reader is encouraged to seek and find faith in the midst of sorrow even if relief has not yet arrived. God loves and provides at all times, even if it may not seem to be so in the short term.

Of course, we have no way of knowing today whether God is bringing adversity and pain into our lives for a specific reason. Assuming we are suffering directly from the hand of God is no more productive than writing the encounter off as "just a coincidence." The only profitable course of action to take is the course we should be taking at all times, whether times are good or bad: Allow God's word to direct us in His ways, and learn the life lessons He brings us along the way.

It is not what God is personally doing or not doing in our daily lives; the important thing is that we use the events of our lives as ways of drawing closer to God and being more like Him. That is the meaning of Paul's words in Romans 8:28—"We know that all things work together for the good of those who love God: those who are called according to His purpose." His "purpose" is not our pain any more than it is our pleasure; it is, as Paul goes on to describe, our calling, our justification, and ultimately our glorification.

1. Is there an appropriate length of time for God to allow us to suffer? If so, when do we know when that time has expired? _____
   _____
   _____
   _____

2. In what sense are the enemies of God's people to be ashamed at the conclusion of the matter (Psa. 6:10)? Is this a resolution we can expect to see in the flesh? What does it mean if we do not see it? _____
   _____
   _____
   _____

3. Define "gracious" in verse 2. What implications do you draw from its use? __
   _____
   _____
   _____

The Drenched Bed

Figure of Speech

Dampening a pillow is one thing; but it would take far more tears than a human body can produce to drench a bed—let alone make it "swim" as is indicated in the New American Standard Bible. Every night the subject of the psalm weeps enough tears to float his bed and dissolve his couch. Perhaps the excessive crying is intended to explain why his eyes "grow old"—or perhaps it refers to the fact that people can show visible signs of age because of emotional trauma, even over a short period of time.

Hyperbole is an extreme exaggeration made for comparative effect. No hungry person could literally eat a horse. It has not literally been forever since you saw a good movie. And clearly the human body cannot produce enough tears to float a bed. But there are days when we have all felt as though the tears would never stop. What a blessing to know God is able to count them all (Psalm 56:8).

---

4. What is your favorite line in the psalm? Why? _____

_____

_____

_____

The Student: A Bible Study

The Absalom story is told in 2 Samuel 13-19—roughly a quarter of the space given to David's entire reign as king over Judah and Israel. It is a story of conflict and rebellion, of promises made and promises broken. Most of all, though, it is a story about a father and a son—of what could have been, and what should have been. And at the end of it, as recorded in 2 Samuel 18:33, and again in 2 Samuel 19:4, the father screams in agony, "My son Absalom! My son, my son Absalom! If only I had died instead of you, Absalom, my son, my son!"

Perhaps David mourned so deeply and so long because he blamed himself for Absalom's downfall. Certainly his performance could have been better along the way. Absalom took it upon himself to avenge his sister, Tamar, by killing his half-brother, Amnon, who had raped, disgraced and then abandoned her. If David had been ruling his house properly, exercising control over his children as a father should, it is reasonable to assume the incident could have been avoided entirely—and if not avoided, then at least mitigated with a proper application of impartial justice.

The rift between Absalom and David widened over the years as David refused to mend fences. By the time David finally welcomed his son back, the seeds appear to have already been planted in his mind to steal the kingdom. His efforts to do so, carried out in front of the entire kingdom, went unchecked by David until he found himself at war with his own son and many of his former lieutenants. And despite David's efforts to spare Absalom's life even in rebellion, David's chief general, Joab, knew Absalom would have to die to put an end to the strife.

David could have done any number of things to avoid this sequence of events. We read in 1 Chronicles 22:6-10 that David made plans with Solomon early on for him to receive the throne and build God's temple in due course of time. However, 1 Kings 1:11-21 indicates David did not make his plans public; worse, his hesitation had empowered Adonijah, another older son, to make a claim for the throne that threatened the lives of Solomon and his mother, Bathsheba. If David had more freely communicated an uncomfortable truth early, he might have avoided the violent deaths of two of his sons. Also, if he had been just with regard to Amnon, he might not have alienated Absalom in the first place.

All parents make mistakes; often they make critical, life-altering ones. There is no going back to choose a better path; the only option we have is to move forward with the wisdom we have acquired, urging our children (as our parents urged us) to learn from our mistakes instead of repeating them.

Read Psalm 6 again—this time with David in mind.

1. How is forgiveness given to a wayward child? Must conditions be met first? What if those conditions are not met? _____
   _____
   _____
   _____

2. Is there a way for us to stop feeling guilty for the mistakes we have made, especially those that have harmed others? _____
   _____
   _____
   _____

Psalm 137—A Parallel Study

Of all the imprecatory psalms (those which invoke ill upon the psalmist's enemies), Psalm 137 may be the most difficult to read. Written in the person of those exiled with Ezekiel by the river Kebar, suffering for the sins of multiple generations as well as their own, the psalm speaks of the Babylonian oppressors coming to them in their sorrow, asking them, "Sing us one of the songs of Zion." Of course, singing joyful songs of their homeland, far away and under foreign rule, was the last thing they wanted to do.

But as justice came to rebellious Jerusalem, so also Babylon was "doomed to destruction." A blessing is placed in verses 8-9 upon the one who participates in the complete destruction of this ungodly and bloodthirsty kingdom.

The brutal nature of the blessing, including the destruction of the children of the Babylonians, seems extreme. Surely killing innocent babies is a horrific act. But you will note that infanticide is not commended specifically; the psalm celebrates the downfall of Babylon and the rise of its destructors, not the specific acts that may have been involved. The psalmist is simply saying the horrors the future kingdom (Persia, as it turned out) would visit upon Babylon would be as terrible as those brought to Judah by Babylon—and that destruction, just as the destruction brought upon Jerusalem, would be an act of God's justice.

1. Explain the difference between a desire for justice and a desire for revenge.
   _____
   _____
   _____

2. Is it difficult to sing "songs of Zion" in our low moments? Should it be? _____
   _____
   _____
   _____

3. Are we on "foreign soil" now as the people of God? What can we do to make it less "foreign?" What can we not do? _____
   _____
   _____
   _____

4. What is your favorite line in the psalm? Why? _____
   _____
   _____
   _____

The Sorrowful: A Case Study

Daria had always dreamed of spending a week in England. Seeing the Royal Guards, visiting Stratford-on-Avon, touring the castles, gaping in amazement at Stonehenge—it would be the trip of a lifetime for her. And with Andrew due to retire in a couple of years, she encouraged him to take as much overtime as possible to maximize his pension from the police department.

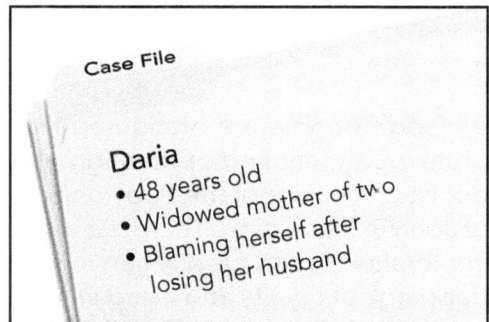

Case File

Daria
- 48 years old
- Widowed mother of two
- Blaming herself after losing her husband

He was shot and killed three months before retirement while trying to detain a drug dealer. It occured on a Saturday night, while her husband worked over-time—overtime she pushed for and wanted.

Suddenly the thought of England was hateful to her. Instead of pining away for a tour of Buckingham Palace, she was thinking of all the evenings watching movies and playing games with Andrew and the boys that she had missed because of his busy work schedule. How he would not see them graduate from college or get married. How she would never see him hold his grandchildren.

"It wasn't your fault," her friends kept insisting, and Daria would nod. "I know, I know," she would say, trying to find comfort. But all she could hear was her own voice in the back of her head. "Yes, it was. Yes, it was. And this is God's way of punishing me for my greed, my dissatisfaction, my presumption.

"I'm sorry, Lord. I'm so, so sorry."

Read Psalm 6 again—this time with Daria in mind.

What would you say to Daria based on Psalm 6? _____
_____
_____
_____

New Testament Insight

> Daughter Babylon, doomed to destruction,
> Happy is the one who pays you back
> What you have done to us.   — Psalm 137:8

Zion is often used metaphorically to refer to the people of God. Isaiah 2:2-3 prophesied that the gospel would go forth from Zion (Jerusalem); this was fulfilled at Pentecost, as recorded in Acts 2. Romans 9:33 and 11:26 also apply the Zion of prophecy to the New Testament kingdom, "the heavenly Jerusalem" (Hebrews 12:22).

As God's people are prefigured in the Old Testament, so is their enemy. The brutal treatment and oppression of God's people in Babylon, as well as the he-donistic behavior of the Babylonians (Daniel 5:1-4), no doubt informs the vision of John in Revelation. There, starting in chapter 17, the epitome of vulgarity and immorality is seen personified in a woman on a scarlet beast, adorned with the trappings of royalty and living in royal luxury—"On her forehead a cryptic name was written: BABYLON THE GREAT THE MOTHER OF PROSTITUTES AND OF THE VILE THINGS OF THE EARTH" (Revelation 17:5).

How Can I Keep from Singing

1. My life flows on in end - less song; A - bove earth's la - men - ta - tion
2. What tho' the tem - pest loud - ly roars? The Lord my Sav - ior liv - eth,
3. I lift my eyes; the cloud grows thin; I see the blue a - bove it;
4. When ty - rants trem - ble in their fear And hear their death knell ring - ing,

I hear the real tho' far off hymn That hails a new cre - a - tion:
And though the dark - ness round me close, Songs in the night He giv - eth.
And day by day this path - way smooths, Since first I learned to love it,
When friends re - joice both far and near, How can I keep from sing - ing?

Thru all the tu - mult and the strife I hear its mu - sic ring - ing;
No storm can shake my in - most calm While to that ref - uge cling - ing.
The peace of Christ makes fresh my heart, A foun - tain ev - er spring - ing;
In pris - on cell and dun - geon vile Our tho'ts to them are wing - ing;

It sounds an ech - o in my soul. How can I keep from sing - ing?
Since Christ is Lord of heav'n and earth, How can I keep from sing - ing?
All things are mine since I am his— How can I keep from sing - ing?
When friends by shame are un - de - filed, How can I keep from sing - ing?

Words: Robert W. Lowry
Music: Robert W. Lowry, st. 4, Doris Plenn

A♭ - 2 - SOL

As the literal Babylon fell, fulfilling the prophecy of Isaiah 14 written decades before even the rise of Nebuchadnezzar, figurative Babylon would also fall, becoming "a dwelling for demons, a haunt for every unclean spirit, a haunt for every unclean bird, and a haunt for every unclean and despicable beast" (Revelation 18:2). The forces of depravity will lose the war against God—in God's time.

The Sorrowful: A Hymn Study

"Always Rejoicing," attributed to "Pauline T," appeared in the *New York Observer* on August 7, 1868. It was first published by Robert Lowry as "How Can I Keep from Singing?" in 1869, when he claimed credit for the music but listed the lyrics as anonymous. Subsequent publications of the hymn further muddy its origins. Lowry himself is credited for the lyrics in some circles.

Folk musician Pete Seeger resurrected it in the 1960s. He learned the song from family friend Doris Plenn, who had penned an additional verse around 1950. The "tyrants" to which she referred were the members of the House Un-American Activities Committee, and those "in prison cell and dungeon vile" were the ones accused of having Communist ties.

Seeger, Plenn, and other musicians in the folk movement typically removed the religious connotations of the hymn when they performed it. Seeger erroneously attributed the song to early American Quakers, prompting modern-day Quakers to adopt it as a sort of unifying anthem.

Irish singer Enya featured "How Can I Keep from Singing?" on her *Shepherd Moons* album in 1991; the song peaked at No. 32 on the UK singles chart. Bruce Springsteen recorded it on *We Shall Overcome: The Seeger Sessions*. Country group SHeDAISY recorded an a cappella version, which re-introduced the religious lyrics so frequently excluded, on their *Brand New Year* Christmas album in 2000. Chris Tomlin credits Lowry and his hymn for inspiring his popular contemporary Christian song, "How Can I Keep from Singing."

The Sorrowful: A Worship Study

We knew Darius and his family were going to be on their way home from his father's funeral the weekend of our study and social, so we did not expect to see them. But there they were, right on time, toting ham and German potato salad that Bianca had made before they left town. And I was grateful that he did; Darius knew "How Can I Keep from Singing" a lot better than I did, and even volunteered to lead it.

"It was a blessing," he said of his father's passing, "both for Dad and for the rest of us. Ever since Mom died, he's been struggling with one health concern after another. He's been in and out of hospitals for two years. He was more than ready to go."

"How are the kids holding up?" I asked. Darius and Bianca have five-year-old twin boys.

"It's tough. They weren't big enough to really miss my mom when she passed, but they got close to Dad this last year when we went back to visit. This was the first funeral they really grasped at all. But we had a nice talk at the graveside. We talked about how much Mom and Dad loved the Lord, and how much they looked forward to going to heaven. It was good."

"You know, you didn't have to come tonight," I told him.

"I know. But I saw the song we were going to focus on tonight, and I just love it so much. And it really spoke to me, where I was emotionally. I felt like, somehow, it would be a denial of my faith, and Dad's faith not to come." And he closed his eyes, smiled, and recited from memory:

> *What though the tempest loudly roars?*
> *The Lord my Savior liveth,*
> *And though the darkness 'round me close,*
> *Songs in the night He giveth.*
> *No storm can shake my inmost calm*
> *While to that rock I'm clinging.*
> *Since Christ is Lord of heav'n and earth,*
> *How can I keep from singing?*

What does "How Can I Keep from Singing" mean to you? _____
_____
_____
_____

The Bible Study Song List

If you were putting a list together for a study about sorrow, what songs would you include? Why? _____
_____
_____
_____

What songs might you exclude? Why? _____
_____
_____
_____

.

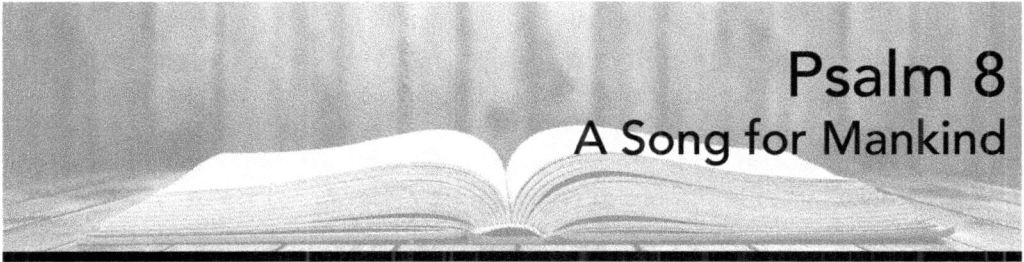

Psalm 8
A Song for Mankind

There are eight planets in our solar system (nine, including Pluto); ours is dwarfed by several of the others. Our sun is only one of an estimated 100-400 billion stars in the Milky Way, a medium-sized galaxy more than 100,000 light-years wide. And the Hubble telescope has revealed that there are probably 100 billion galaxies, perhaps even 200 billion, in the universe. And if the magnificent things we see in our own tiny part of that immense cosmos is any indication at all, the number of truly awe-inspiring things that God has made must literally border on the infinite.

And yet, in all of this marvelous creation, it is mankind that hold God's heart. Only mankind.

Even with the limited view David has of the cosmos, he is astounded at the vastness of "Your heavens, the work of Your fingers, the moon and stars which You set in place." And he is humbled that human beings such as himself, with all of our frailties, weaknesses and limitations, should be the aspect in all of creation that would be considered special to God. His psalm is not intended to degrade man as an infinitely miniscule and insignificant speck on the cosmic spectrum; exactly the opposite, in fact. He tells us by inspiration that it is humanity and only humanity that is the center of creation.

The idea of covering the heavens with His majesty (v.1) calls to mind the imagery from Psalm 19:4-6. In that passage the sun is depicted as a runner, endlessly looping around a track that encompasses the entire world.

¹ LORD, our Lord,
how magnificent is Your name
  throughout the earth!
You have covered the heavens
  with Your majesty.
² Because of Your adversaries,
You have established a
  stronghold
from the mouths of children and
  nursing infants,
to silence the enemy and the
  avenger.
³ When I observe Your heavens,
the work of Your fingers,
the moon and the stars,
which You set in place,
⁴ what is man that You remember
  Him,
the son of man that You look
  after him?
⁵ You made him little less than
  God
and crowned with glory and
  honor.
⁶ You made him lord over the
  works of Your hands;
You put everything under his
  feet,
⁷ all the sheep and oxen,
as well as animals in the wild,
⁸ birds of the sky,
and fish of the sea
passing through the curtains of
  the seas.
⁹ LORD, our Lord,
how magnificent is Your name
  throughout the earth!

Everything it touches sees the glory of the One who made all things. Likewise here in this psalm, the glory of God swallows the creation whole. The idea of God being immense enough to have a garment larger than the sky boggles the mind; having that garment made out of "majesty," whatever that might look like, just makes us all the more in awe of Him.

From the beginning, God gave men and women stewardship over the created world. We may differ on exactly how to best "subdue" (Genesis 1:28) the earth, but respect for the Bible requires that we accept the principle that mankind is separate from the rest of creation and superior to it. The earth is here to serve our interests, and not the other way around.

1. Explain how testimony of God's greatness can come "from the mouths of children and nursing infants." _____
   _____
   _____
   _____

2. What is the "glory and honor" mankind receives from God? How can mankind maximize it? _____
   _____
   _____
   _____

3. At what point, if any, does stewardship of the physical world become cruel and inappropriate? _____
   _____
   _____
   _____

4. What is your favorite line in the psalm? Why? _____
   _____
   _____
   _____

Mankind: A Bible Study

If Rome was the political center of the world in the First Century, Athens was the intellectual center. People traveled from every nation to discuss anything and everything with the greatest thinkers of the age. Plato, Aristotle, and a host of other worthies called Athens home. And the Areopagus, named after the Greek god of war, Ares, was an ironic location for many of the greatest intellectual battles.

The Name of God

Figure of Speech

The Tetragrammaton, YHWH, was sacred to the Israelites. It was only written with a freshly dipped pen; no chance would be taken that it would be written in a ragged fashion. But the care taken in its writing was nothing compared to the care taken in its speaking. So fearful that they might violate the third commandment, YHWH was rarely spoken at all.

Names connoted power in the ancient world. By using the name of God, an Israelite saw himself as bringing God into his presence. To do so in a trivial, let alone disrespectful, way was unthinkable. It is no wonder that the "profane" (that is, the non-spiritual) came to mean that which is unholy.

Praising the "name," then, is to praise God Himself. Calling on His name for salvation is to trust God, and God alone, to save. To use such a magnificent name inappropriately—to testify falsely by it, or to attach it to that which is unholy, or even to use it casually or irreverently—is to "misuse the name" and to bring upon oneself the penalty for doing so (Exodus 20:7).

This is where Paul was brought to discuss the strange religious doctrine he had been sharing with the Jews and other believers in Jehovah over a period of time. As Acts 17:21 tells us, "Now all the Athenians and the foreigners residing there spent their time on nothing else but telling or hearing something new." And Paul was more than willing to share with them the greatest knowledge the world had ever seen.

Humankind is uniquely suited for intellectual development. We are intelligent, self-aware, moral, planning, emotional, serving beings. Nothing in the animal kingdom, however advanced, can come close to paralleling our capabilities. But this capacity was given to us for a specific reason: to empower us in our search for God. Paul appealed to this sense of discovery in his sermon at the Areopagus. He pointed out the fact that the Athenians had been moved even to serve "an unknown god" (Acts 17:23). And in fact, the god they did not know was the one God who was truly worthy of service.

Man left to himself can perceive evidences of God, but he is limited by his imagination. It is natural to think of God in terms of gold, silver and stone, but the true God is nothing like anything man can imagine. It requires revelation to tell us of His true nature. The greatest accomplishment of man is not to do something remarkable, but rather to realize what he cannot possibly do and to build faith in the God who does all.

Read Psalm 8 again—this time with Paul in mind.

1. What does it mean to you that God "is not far from each one of us?" _____

_____

_____

_____

2. How can elevated human thought interfere with pursuing the knowledge of God?_____

_____

_____

_____

Psalm 127—A Parallel Study

Whatever pursuit any of us may assign ourselves, it will come to nothing eventually if it leaves out God. Even though we put in as many hours as the clock will permit, work our fingers to the bone, and perhaps even achieve great things in the short term, God can bring it all down in a moment. And He will do exactly that in due course of time for all those who lived their lives in the prideful pursuit of selfish ambition.

The pursuit can be as grand as nation-building or as mundane as a single house. But God is the ruler of all; forces great and small, near and distant, are under His domain. The degree of confidence we can and should place in God dwarfs all else; if we are so negligent as to ignore the help God offers us, why bother posting any watchman at all?

The image of a house is extended in the second half of the psalm, as we are told that even the heritage of children is about our connection to God. He blesses us as He sees fit, and He trusts that we will use our role as parents (if we are so blessed) to perpetuate a reverence for the Giver of all blessings (James 1:17).

1. What "house" (or houses) does the Lord help us build? How might we try to build them without His help? _____

_____

_____

_____

2. Read verse 2 in a variety of translations. Put your understanding of the verse in your own words below. _____

_____

_____

_____

3. How are children like arrows? _____

_____

_____

_____

4. What is your favorite line in the psalm? Why? _____

_____

_____

_____

Mankind: A Case Study

When asked to write a paper for science class on Nicolaus Copernicus, Penny was excited. Writing was one of her best skills, and she excelled at research. Plus, it was an opportunity to mend fences with her teacher, Ms. Adams. Ever since Penny had questioned the theory of evolution from a Biblical perspective, she had gotten the impression that Ms. Adams considered her somehow "anti-science." She was eager to prove Ms. Adams wrong.

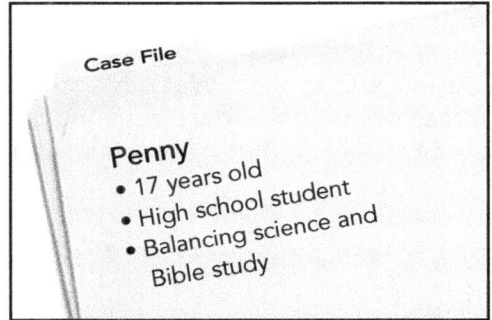

Case File

Penny
- 17 years old
- High school student
- Balancing science and Bible study

After reading her report in front of the class and sitting down, Ms. Adams asked, "So, why was Copernicus so hesitant to publish his theory while he was still living?"

"He knew the opposition he would face from the Pope and the Catholic establishment, and I suppose he wasn't willing to stand up and be counted for what he believed was the truth. Actually, I came away from my research a little disappointed in Copernicus that he did not have the courage to defend his position."

"But in the end, Copernicus was proved right and the Bible was proved wrong," said Ms. Adams, with a bit of a smirk.

"No," Penny replied patiently. "His detractors, including prominent figures in the Catholic church, were proved wrong. The Bible never says the earth is the physical center of the universe."

"Of course it does!" said Ms. Adams, incredulous. "There are plenty of passages that mention the earth standing still, and the sun traveling across the sky from east to west."

"But people talk like that even today. Those are figures of speech. I don't know whether people in Bible times understood the workings of the world properly or not, and I don't see why it matters either way. They trusted God to tell them the things they needed to know, and so do I."

"So you're saying we should accept the Bible and reject science?"

"No, I'm saying the Bible isn't a science book and shouldn't be read like one. I don't read the Bible to learn about science. I read it to learn about God and my place in the universe. And the Bible says I am at the center of it—the spiritual center, not the physical center.

"To me, that makes everything I learn through science that much more amazing—that God would set all these forces in motion and keep them in motion, forces we are only now beginning to understand. Really, the more I understand about the world through science, the more I believe in the God who made it all."

Read Psalm 8 again—this time with Penny in mind.

What would you say to Penny based on Psalm 8? _____
_____
_____

New Testament Insight

> You made him little less than God
> and crowned him with glory and honor. — Psalm 8:5

The status of human beings in relation to the rest of the created world is unrivaled. Being made in the image of God (Genesis 1:27), we can claim a connection to the Creator that no other aspect of creation can, no matter how wondrous or inexplicable.

The term "son of man" occurs only eight times in the Old Testament outside of the book of Ezekiel, in which it is used 84 times to refer to the prophet himself. All of these passages refer to human beings. But "Son of Man" occurs 83 times in the gospels, all referring to Jesus. He uses it as a claim to deity (John 9:35); He attaches it to heavenly glory at the beginning of His ministry (John 1:51) and at His death (Luke 22:48, 69). Stephen refers to Jesus as "the Son of Man" when he sees Him standing at the right hand of the Father (Acts 7:56). Clearly it is a term Jesus used to claim deity and humanity simultaneously.

The "son of man" in Hebrews 2:5-8, which quotes Psalm 8, refers to man's oversight of the created world; all is subjected to him. But a connection is made

Dear Lord and Father of Mankind

1. Dear Lord and Father of mankind, Forgive our foolish ways;
Re-clothe us in our rightful mind, In purer lives Thy service find,
In deeper rev-'rence, praise.

2. In simple trust like theirs who heard, Beside the Syrian sea,
The gracious calling of the Lord, Let us, like them, without a word,
Rise up and follow Thee.

3. Drop Thy still dews of quietness Till all our strivings cease;
Take from our souls the strain and stress, And let our ordered lives confess
The beauty of Thy peace.

Words: John G. Whittier
Music: Frederick C. Maker

D - 4 - M

in verse 9 to Jesus, "the Son of Man," who assumed human form temporarily. The Septuagint, quoted in Hebrews, uses the word for angels instead of the related word for God when referring to Jesus' status on earth. The point is not that Jesus was less than angels or even than God on earth (Colossians 2:9), but that He occupied a lowly status before being crowned King of kings "so that by God's grace He might taste death for everyone."

Mankind: A Hymn Study

"Dear Lord and Father of Mankind" is about drugs. Really.

John Greenleaf Whittier was one of the "fireside poets," a group known for verses with regular meter, common themes, and rhymed stanzas. They were the first American poets who found widespread popularity even in Europe.

Whittier, a Quaker, rejected the growing tendency among the idle rich to find satisfaction in the growing drug trade from the East. *The Brewing of Soma* is a poem Whittier wrote in 1872. Several of the verses of that poem were put to music to become the hymn we know. *The Brewing of Soma* tells of priests brewing and drinking soma, a sacred drink thought to possess hallucinogenic properties, in an attempt to achieve a sort of divine status. Whittier's Quaker roots are shown as the libidinous lifestyle of soma is rejected for a simple life of pursuing God in God's way. Thus God helps "reclothe us in our rightful mind." The spectacular is exchanged for the "soft whisper" of God's presence as Elijah experienced in 1 Kings 19:11-12. Whittier makes the connection more clearly in a stanza not generally included in our hymnals:

> *Breathe through the heat of our desire*
> *Thy coolness and Thy balm;*
> *Let sense be dumb; let flesh retire;*
> *Speak through the earthquake, wind, and fire*
> *O still, small voice of calm.*

Frederick Charles Maker composed the tune typically sung in the United States to go with Whittier's poem. Maker, born in 1844 in Bristol, England, served as an organist for several nonconformist churches during his adulthood, and also worked as a professor of music at Clifton College. Other compositions of Maker's accompany hymns such as "Beneath the Cross of Jesus" and "O Sacred Head." He died January 1, 1927.

Mankind: A Worship Study

"Most of you are aware of my past," Adrian said. "For those who don't, I was addicted to cocaine for years. I still am, I suppose, although I've been clean and sober for …" He stopped for a moment to calculate. "Four years, two months and five days," he finished, finally, to the congratulations of all.

"I took drugs because I was not satisfied with myself. And I don't mean like you might want to lose another ten pounds or get a college degree. No, I felt restricted. I was confined in a human prison. I read biographies of people like Timothy Leary and Jim Morrison. I dabbled in occultism. I tried anything and everything to … what did I call it? 'Maximize my human and superhuman potential.' That's what I called it.

"Don't let anyone tell you Ouija boards and tarot cards are harmless. That's how I got started. I wanted to assume control of my present and my future. And anything that offered me hope of achieving that, I was willing to give it a try."

"Contentment," I said. "You couldn't find it."

"Exactly right. Contentment was completely foreign to me. Not only did I not have it, I didn't want it. Life was all about more, more, more. Bigger and better.

"Then one day my mother came to visit while I was faking my way through rehab. And I will never forget this. She looked me in the eye, with tears in hers, and said, 'When did you become so selfish?' And I had never thought of myself that way. But she was exactly right. The price my family had to pay for my excess, the threat I had become to my friends, the burden I had become to society—none of it had ever crossed my mind. All I had ever thought of was how to get more for myself. Nothing about anyone else.

"So I got my Bible out, for the first time in a long time. I started studying about service, and pride, and hope. And contentment," he added, pointing at me. "I started seeing life as a way of properly using what God had given me, and not being caught up in finding what I didn't have, what might not even exist.

"My first Sunday back, we sang 'Dear Lord and Father of Mankind.' I remember wishing the sermon would be short so I could hurry up and confess my sins to everyone. I never knew humility could feel so good."

"Did you stop wanting drugs after that?" someone asked.

"I wish!" he replied, chuckling. "No, drugs are like sin, I think. The desire is always there. And the opportunity to drift back into old habits is always there. But I definitely find myself thinking less about drugs and everything drugs brought me. It seems like the longer I devote myself to holier things, the less appeal the unholy things have."

"Sounds like pretty good advice regarding sin in general," I suggested.

What does "Dear Lord and Father of Mankind" mean to you? _____
_____
_____
_____

The Bible Study Song list

If you were putting a list together for a study about mankind, what songs would you include? Why? _____

_____

_____

What songs might you exclude? Why? _____

_____

_____

Psalm 10
A Song for the Doubter

Faith is not always easy. We tend to have preconceived ideas, often based in Scripture, of how God will respond to our adversity and subsequent prayers. And when He fails to act "appropriately," we begin to wonder whether our service to God is really accomplishing anything. Does God really care about us? Does He really have the knowledge of our pain and the ability to alleviate it? And if so, why hasn't He?

Making it far worse is the fact that our detractors, those who do not honor God and perhaps even scorn Him, profit from His hesitation. They are further emboldened to pursue their wicked ways, often at our expense. We have more and more difficulty seeing the plan.

But then, it's not our plan to see; it's God's. And our enemies are not ultimately accountable to us, but to Him. It's not our place to take God's place by determining what requires His immediate attention.

So in truth, it is not just our sense of God's justice that is being challenged; these circumstances challenge the very core of our faith. Does God reward? Does God provide? Does God avenge? Does God even exist?

It is entirely appropriate for us to ask God for validation in this life; the Psalms and other passages of Scripture are replete with examples of such prayers. But we also know that hesitation does not equate to abandonment. Jesus' parables suggest that God may be hoping that we use His hesitation to grow even more insistent, and by extension more dependent, on prayer (Luke 11:5-9, 18:1-8). The point of prayer,

¹ LORD, why do You stand so far away?
Why do You hide in times of trouble?
² In arrogance the wicked relentlessly pursue the afflicted;
let them be caught in the schemes they have devised.
³ For the wicked one boasts about his own cravings,
the one who is greedy curses and despises the LORD.
⁴ In all his scheming,
the wicked arrogantly thinks:
"There is no accountability,
since God does not exist."
⁵ His ways are always secure;
Your lofty judgments are beyond his sight;
he scoffs at all his adversaries.
⁶ He says to himself, "I will never be moved—
from generation to generation without calamity."
⁷ Cursing deceit, and violence fill his mouth;
trouble and malice are under his tongue.
⁸ He waits in ambush near the villages;
he kills the innocent in secret places;
his eyes are on the lookout for the helpless.

9 He lurks in secret like a lion in a thicket.

He lurks in order to seize the afflicted.

He seizes the afflicted and drags him in his net.

10 He crouches and bends down;

the helpless fall because of his strength.

11 He says to himself, "God has forgotten;

He hides His face and will never see."

12 Rise up, LORD God! Lift up Your hand.

Do not forget the afflicted.

13 Why has the wicked despised God?

He says to himself, "You will not demand an account."

14 But You Yourself have seen trouble and grief,

observing it in order to take the matter into Your hands.

The helpless entrusts himself to You;

You are a helper of the fatherless.

15 Break the arm of the wicked and evil person;

call his wickedness into account

until nothing remains of it.

16 The LORD is King forever and ever;

the nations will perish from His land.

17 LORD, You have heard the desire of the humble;

You will strengthen their hearts.

You will listen carefully,

18 doing justice for the fatherless and the oppressed,

so that men of the earth may terrify them no more.

after all, is not to "get stuff." No, it is to remind us of our dependence upon God; of His sovereignty, holiness and power; of our responsibility to pursue His will in our life over our own, just as Jesus did (Matthew 26:39). Therefore we should not be discouraged if His response is not exactly what we would have wished, since our own will was never the objective in the first place.

In the end, as verse 16 reminds us, "The LORD is King forever and ever." He may not always act in the way we think a king should act; but then, the King does not answer to us. We, like the psalmist, can fall back on the assurance that God is "doing justice for the fatherless and the oppressed so that men of the earth may terrify them no more" (v.18)—whether or not it ever occurs within our immediate vision. The King reigns.

1. Why might God's inaction appear to us that He is standing "so far away?" ___

   _____
   _____
   _____
   _____
   _____
   _____

2. How destructive to the cause of Christ is it when the "bad guys" are perceived to be winning in the short term? _____

   _____
   _____
   _____
   _____
   _____

3. Explain from verse 13 how a lack of accountability emboldens the sinner. Make application with regard to accountability in other contexts. _____

   _____
   _____
   _____
   _____
   _____

Like a Lion	Figure of Speech

"The king of beasts" once lived in large numbers in Israel, particularly the lush Jordan valley. And although attacks on healthy humans were likely as uncommon then as now, it did happen. It was not unusual at all for a weak or injured individual away from the safety of home to meet his final end at the paw of a lion. The traveling Jew in Jesus' parable in Luke 10:30-35, for instance, likely would have wound up dying in a lion attack.

Although the majesty of the lion is sometimes applied to the things of God (most notably Revelation 5:5), it is more commonly found in the Bible to refer either to literal lion attacks (1 Samuel 17:34-37, 1 Kings 13:24-28) or to figurative assaults on God's people, either from other humans (Psalm 22:13) or from the devil himself (1 Peter 5:8). Sometimes the attack on God's people comes from God Himself with the wrath and power of a lion (Amos 5:18-19). In that terrifying day, hopefully, "His children will come trembling" (Hosea 11:10) and not, as one might expect, run and hide from Him.

4. What is your favorite line in the psalm? Why? _____
_____
_____

The Doubter: A Bible Study

We have a tendency to think men and women who were directly inspired by God, who walked and talked with God in ways we cannot possibly understand, were somehow immune to doubt. If this is the case with Old Testament prophets, surely it would be even more so for the one of whom Jesus said, "I assure you: Among those born of women no one greater than John the Baptist has appeared" (Matthew 11:11).

It is difficult to read Matthew 11:1-6 in any way other than John is wavering in his faith. Remember, John witnessed the testimony of the Spirit at Jesus' baptism, and heard the voice from heaven say, "This is My beloved Son. I take delight in Him!" (Matthew 3:17). John turned his own disciples away from himself and toward Jesus, saying, "He must increase, but I must decrease" (John 3:30).

But months had passed since then, and Jesus' kingdom had not been revealed yet. Worse, John himself was languishing in Herod's prison for condemning his adulterous marriage (Matthew 14:3-4). Whatever John anticipated out of Jesus, surely it was not this.

We must remember, prophecy was given in piecemeal fashion, not all at once as in the modern day with our modern Bibles (1 Corinthians 13:9-10). And there is no indication in the text that John understood the spiritual nature of the coming kingdom any more than the rest of Jesus' contemporaries did. So when we read of John sending a deputation from prison to Jesus to ask, "Are You the One who is to come, or should we expect someone else?" (Matthew 11:3), it may be exactly what it appears to be—John had gotten so caught up in his deplorable circumstances and perceived abandonment that he had begun to doubt his own prophecy.

Certainly Jesus' response does not seem to have a disappointed or betrayed tone to it: "Go and report to John what you hear and see: the blind see, the lame walk, those with skin diseases are healed, the deaf hear, the dead are raised, and the poor are told the good news. And if anyone is not offended because of Me, he is blessed" (Matthew 11:4-6). His point is, His Lordship is not denied because our expectations of the Lord are not realized. His Lordship is affirmed every time He shows the power of God in His behavior, or the wisdom of God in His speech, or the love of God in His compassion. It is not He who should be expected to adjust His behavior; it is we who should be expected to adjust our vision of what a Lord is and what a Lord should do.

Read Psalm 10 again—this time with John in mind.

1. Who won the confrontation between John and Herod in the eyes of the average observer? Who really won? _____
_____
_____
_____

2. Do you think John's heart was strengthened in prison prior to his death? How?
_____
_____
_____
_____

Psalm 95—A Parallel Study

We have a choice between joy and misery, between faith and doubt. Israel in the wilderness should teach us this. The very names of Meribah ("quarreling") and Massah ("testing") remind us as they reminded Israel of old that circumstances will try our faith from time to time. We may ask, as they did, "Is the LORD among us or not?" (Exodus 17:7). And He will be as disgusted with us as He was with them if we forget to give Him praise in the midst of our sorrows. By choosing to "shout joyfully to the LORD" (Psalm 95:1) in times of tribulation instead of lashing out at Him for treating us so poorly, we remind ourselves that, even on our worst day, the blessings we receive from the God of heaven are incalculable and unfathomable.

Paul exhorts in 1 Corinthians 10:6, with regard to rebellious Israel of old, "Now these things became examples for us, so that we will not desire evil as they did." Hopefully we can heed Paul's warnings better than Israel of old heeded Moses'.

1. Is there a difference between singing to God and "shouting" to Him? Explain.

_____

_____

_____

_____

2. What is implied in the fact that God owns "the depths of the earth...the mountain peaks...the sea...[and] the dry land" (v.4-5)? _____

_____

_____

_____

3. What caused Israel to murmur, both at Meribah and Massah and at other occasions? How does their murmuring compare to our murmuring today? _____

_____

_____

_____

4. What is your favorite line in the psalm? Why? _____

_____

_____

_____

The Doubter: A Case Study

No one would have predicted ten years earlier that Jana would still be unmarried. And they told Jana that. Frequently. Of course, that didn't make Jana any more content with her situation.

Case File

Jana
• 29 years old
• Single, no children
• Concerned she may never get married

"Maybe I was too picky," she said to her father halfway through her usual Saturday pint of chocolate chip ice cream. "Several of the Christians I dated in college are looking a lot better than they did back then."

"Well, there's no point in reliving all of that," Dad said. "You had your reasons—and personally, I thought you were too good for any of them. Not that you are surprised at all that Proud Papa would take that position."

Jana smiled a bit. "Thanks, Dad. But the reality is, I have been holding out hope all my life for a godly man to come along who would hold the same values I did, who loves kids like I do, who would be able to get the most out of me as

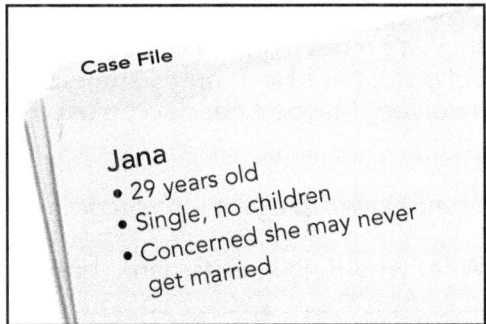

a Christian and who I could build up as well. But I have to be honest: the guys I dated who I liked best, who understood me best, were not Christians."

"Really?"

"And I know it's not ideal at all. I absolutely want to marry a Christian. But I also absolutely want to get married. I want kids. I don't want Mom to be bugging me every Thanksgiving about getting her some grandchildren."

"But you don't want to compromise your faith in pursuit of physical things, no matter how wonderful those physical things might be. I can work on your mother."

"Well, thanks for that," she said with a slightly teary smile. "And you're right— God has to come first. But it doesn't have to be an either-or thing. Christians marry non-Christians all the time. And sure, it doesn't always work. But it doesn't always work when you marry a Christian, either."

"But it makes sense to set yourself up for success, right?"

"Of course. But the Christian man at 25 is not the Christian he is at 45, or 65. He grows. He develops. And a non-Christian is going to do the same thing. Surely the most important thing is to get someone with good character, who will support me in my walk with Christ—and of course, join me in it. But maybe it's not reasonable to require him to get 80 percent of it right on day one. After all, husbands become Christians. Wives become Christians."

"So how would you suggest going about finding this non-Christian Mr. Right?"

"Well, I'm not going to start trolling the bars, if that's what you're asking. No, I think it's more a matter of being open to possibilities. In the past, at work and in college, I have been pretty straightforward about not being interested in getting involved. Maybe I need to adjust that a bit."

Read Psalm 10 again—this time with Jana in mind.

What would you say to Jana, based on Psalm 10? _____
_____
_____
_____

New Testament Insight

"So I swore in My anger,
'They will not enter My rest.' "   — Psalm 95:11

The "rest" on the other side of the Jordan was denied to the rebellious generation of Israelites in the wilderness. Instead of taking hope in what God promised was in store for them in just a little while, they chose to live in the present. So

Abide with Me

1. A - bide with me; fast falls the e - ven - tide;
2. Swift to its close ebbs out life's lit - tle day;
3. Come not in ter - rors, as the King of kings,
4. I need Thy pres - ence eve - ry pass - ing hour.
5. I fear no foe with Thee at hand to bless;
6. Hold Thou Thy cross be - fore my clos - ing eyes;

The dark - ness deep - ens; Lord with me a - bide.
Earth's joys grow dim; its glo - ries pass a - way.
But kind and good, with heal - ing in Thy wings,
What but Thy grace can foil the tempt - er's pow'r?
Ills have no weight, and tears no bit - ter - ness.
Shine through the gloom and point me to the skies.

When oth - er help - ers fail and com - forts flee,
Change and de - cay in all a - round I see;
Tears for all woes, a heart for eve - ry plea—
Who like Thy - self my guide and stay can be?
Where is death's sting? Where, grave, thy vic - to - ry?
Heav'n's morn - ing breaks, and earth's vain shad - ows flee;

Help of the help - less, O a - bide with me.
O Thou who chang - est not, a - bide with me.
Come, Friend of sin - ners, thus a - bide with me.
Through cloud and sun - shine, Lord, a - bide with me.
I tri - umph still, if Thou a - bide with me.
In life, in death, O Lord, a - bide with me.

Words: Henry F. Lyte
Music: William H. Monk

Eb - 4 - MI

God left them there, to live and eventually die in the reality they faithlessly chose for themselves. They wound up working far more hard for their life in the wilderness than their children would for their life in Canaan.

Joshua's leadership across the Jordan prefigured the deliverance from sin's wilderness given by his namesake. Jesus, whose name is the Aramaic equivalent of "Joshua," provides a respite from the rigors of sin. The writer of Hebrews makes the connection between Psalm 95:7-11 and the gospel. "A Sabbath rest remains, therefore, for God's people. For the person who has entered His rest has rested from his own works, just as God did from His. Let us then make every effort to enter that rest, so that no one will fall into the same pattern of disobedience" (Hebrews 4:9-11).

The promise of heaven lies in front of us just as Canaan did for Israel of old. When we sing songs about crossing over Jordan, we are acknowledging that we are mere wanderers in the wilderness here—that our true home awaits us, where the troubles and pain that so completely dominate our lives now will no longer afflict us. We will truly, finally, be at rest (Revelation 14:13).

The Doubter: A Hymn Study

Henry Francis Lyte and his wife, Ann, worked with a church in a small fishing town in Devonshire, England, for 23 years until tuberculosis finally forced Henry to step aside. He preached his final sermon on September 4, 1847. After preaching, he took a walk on the beach near his home, then retired to his room. He emerged an hour later and handed the lyrics to "Abide with Me" to Ann.

Soon after his retirement he took a trip to southern Europe for his health. While there he mailed a revision of the hymn back home to Ann. Three weeks later, he passed away. A preacher waiting on him in his final hours said his final words were, "Peace! Joy!" It was sung for the first time at Lyte's memorial service, with accompanying music penned by Lyte himself.

"Abide with Me" achieved great popularity in its day and remains one of the most beloved hymns in the world a century and a half later. Although it has been sung to a variety of tunes through the years, by far the most familiar is "Eventide" by William H. Monk. It is this rendition that was sung at the weddings of King George VI and Queen Elizabeth II of the United Kingdom. It is sung as a part of numerous events and celebrations in the UK, including before kick-off before every FA Cup Final soccer match since 1927. It was also sung at the opening ceremonies of the 2012 Summer Olympics in London.

The Doubter: A Worship Study

Jack was not one of our regulars. He would have good days and bad days. The good days often resulted in him coming to the study and sharing his good news; often it would not. The bad days typically resulted in him staying home and, to put it bluntly, feeling sorry for himself.

The night we focused on "Abide with Me," not surprisingly, was one of the nights he missed. And it was unfortunate, since I spent most of the evening thinking about him.

I snagged him the next Sunday and got him to go out to lunch with me and the family. Naturally I expressed my regret at his absence at the study; naturally he took the opportunity to regale me with the depth and breadth of his difficulties.

"But, see, that's my point," I said when I could fit a word in. "The times of desperation, the times of doubt—those are the times we need to lean on God that much more. 'Abide with me.' It's not just asking God to drop in for a visit on Sundays, or asking Him to let us visit Him. It's a lifelong commitment."

"Yes, but I have to say, I wonder sometimes how committed God is to me. I look and look for Him in my daily difficulties. And I can't find Him."

I grabbed his shoulder and looked him in the eye. "I'll be honest, Jack—I think you're kidding yourself. I don't think you're looking for God at all. I think you're looking for solutions."

"Isn't it the same thing?"

"Not the way you define 'solutions.' God isn't promising a way around the hardship. He is promising you something much better—to guide you through the hardship, to give you purpose and hope, to build your faith so one day you will be ready to receive the greatest blessing He has to give—the one he reserves for the truly faithful."

What does "Abide with Me" mean to you? _____
_____
_____
_____

The Bible Study Song list

If you were putting a list together for a study about doubt, what songs would you include? Why? _____
_____
_____

What songs might you exclude? Why? _____
_____
_____

Psalm 14
A Song for the Faithless

One is a fool who explains the marvelous creation he sees every day with a philosophy that denies God. The miracle of human existence, the amazing balance of nature, the infinite vastness of space, it all bears His divine fingerprints.

Equally foolish is the one who chooses not to seek after God. Perhaps he is convinced the question of God's existence is unanswerable and therefore irrelevant. Or perhaps he gives lip service to the presence of God but imagines Him to be a distant, disengaged God who cares little for the actions of mankind.

The fool is foolish because he has chosen a foolish path. He is pursuing sin in his life, and he has convinced himself that God doesn't see, doesn't care, or doesn't exist. It is easy to convince yourself of the "truth" of a matter when it allows you to do what you have already decided to do.

When our decisions for life exclude the possibility of God, and by extension the possibility of long-term accountability, depravity naturally ensues. Ephesians 2:3 says that before Jesus "by nature we were children under wrath, as the others were also." It was not a "nature" thrust upon us by forces beyond our control; we worked hard to acquire our evil habits. And a life that makes no attempt to pursue holiness is doomed to find itself steeped in wickedness very quickly.

It would be tragic enough if that were the end of the story—sinful, godless souls doomed to destruction. But the faithful, those who acknowledge and serve their Creator, find

[1] The fool says in his heart,
"God does not exist."
They are corrupt; their actions
are revolting.
There is no one who does
good.
[2] The LORD looks down from
heaven on the human race
to see if there is one who is
wise,
one who seeks God.
[3] All have turned away;
All alike have become corrupt.
There is no one who does
good,
not even one.
[4] Will evildoers never understand?
They consume my people as
they consume bread;
they do not call on the LORD.
[5] Then they will be filled with
terror;
for God is with those who are
righteous.
[6] You sinners frustrate the
plans of the afflicted,
but the LORD is his refuge.
[7] Oh, that Israel's deliverance
would come from Zion!
When the LORD restores His
captive people,
Jacob will rejoice; Israel will
be glad.

themselves stymied frequently by the faithless. Rarely is it enough for the godless one to keep his godlessness to himself; no, he must convert the godly or interfere as much as he can with the pursuits of the godly.

We hope and pray for the salvation of such souls. But we also pray for ourselves, as the people of God. We pray that God delivers us from having to deal with the naysayers and doubters in this life. But whether we are delivered or not, we pray most of all that we not lose faith ourselves, that we find the strength to persevere in times of trial.

The definition of "good" causes trouble for some. In a Biblical context, "good" is defined by the good God; "good" things are those that comply with His vision for them. That is why creation was "good" in the beginning; prior to the fall, it had not been tarnished by man and his sin. But the unbeliever, in lieu of God's definitions, makes up his own. And not surprisingly, "good" tends strongly to be defined in such a way as to flatter the one writing the definition. Extended discussions about whether a sinner's "good" deeds are as meaningful and sincere as those of a Christian miss the point entirely. It is not a matter of improving society or achieving some professed moral good with our actions; "good" deeds are those that glorify God. And although none but God Himself can do that perfectly (Luke 18:19), we can and must pursue goodness (Galatians 5:22) through the working of the Spirit in our lives—and engage in the "good works" (Ephesians 2:10) that goodness inspires. By God's grace, that will be "good" enough.

1. Is it possible for a soul to be beyond redemption? Explain your answer. _____
   _____
   _____
   _____

2. What should our attitude of heart be toward those who deny God? _____
   _____
   _____
   _____

3. Why does God allow faithlessness to exist? List examples of when God did not allow it to exist. Suggest reasons why He does not act similarly today. __
   _____
   _____
   _____

4. What is your favorite line in the psalm? Why? _____
   _____
   _____
   _____

Eating People Like Bread

Figure of Speech

Virtually every reference to something being "consumed" in the Bible specifies fire as the consuming element. This is one of a small handful of passages (Psalm 27:2 and Nahum 3:12 are others) in which people are metaphorically eaten by other people. The intent to destroy for personal benefit is obvious in the imagery.

It need not be the overt enemies of the people of God who "eat" them, though. Paul warns the Galatians about "brethren" who, so consumed with their fleshly desires, will turn on their spiritual family. "But if you bite and devour one another, watch out, or you will be consumed by one another" (Galatians 5:15). Love for our neighbor, and certainly our brethren, should keep such things from ever occurring; if we see ourselves hurting one another, we need to stop, repent, and make amends before we do permanent damage to the body of Christ.

The Faithless: A Bible Study

The surname of Elymas is ironic. He was called Bar-Jesus, meaning his father had been named Jesus. But he had no connection to our Lord, Jesus of Nazareth, at all—quite the opposite, in fact. The apostle Paul called him, "You son of the Devil, full of all deceit and all fraud, enemy of all righteousness" (Acts 13:10).

Paul's reaction was so strong because Elymas not only refused to listen to the gospel message Paul and Barnabas had brought to Selucia, on the island of Cyprus; he was deliberately interfering with their efforts to teach Sergius Paulus, who was serving there as proconsul. This grated at Paul, and not just because of one Bible study; surely Paul understood the benefits of having strong relations with someone of Paulus' position. As valuable as a single soul was, and is, Paulus could have paved the way for a smoother course of the gospel throughout the island, perhaps leading to dozens if not hundreds of conversions.

Elymas was no more interested in the souls of others than he was in his own. Clearly he saw Paul and Barnabas as interlopers, interfering with the relationship with the proconsul that he, no doubt, had worked long and hard to establish. Of course, Paul cared nothing for Elymas' efforts toward political and social prominence. But when they interfered with the salvation of souls, he would not stand for it. He struck him with temporary but total blindness, forcing him to be led about by the hand. Paulus saw it all and was moved to believe in the gospel—not, according to the text, because of Paul's power, but because he was "astonished at the teaching about the Lord" (Acts 13:12). The power of the gospel is stronger than any experience for the true believer.

Being willingly blind to the glory of God and His Son Jesus Christ is far worse than any physical affliction. The old saying is true (though not Biblical, as many assume): there are none so blind as those who will not see. Paul writes of the Gentile world in Romans 1:21, "For though they knew God, they did not glorify Him as God or show gratitude. Instead, their thinking became nonsense, and their senseless minds were darkened." Further complicating matters, religious men who are presumed, both by themselves and by society, often are really "blind guides" (Matthew 23:16), making it more difficult instead of more convenient for lost souls to find their way to Christ.

Thankfully, Jesus came into the world to be "a light for the nations" (Isaiah 49:6). Because of Him, "the light of the world" (John 8:12, 9:5), we have the opportunity to find our way to a right relationship with God.

Read Psalm 14 again—this time with Elymas in mind.

1. List some other Bible texts where blindness or darkness is used to refer to separation from God. Is the separation God's doing or man's doing? _____
   _____
   _____
   _____

2. Discuss the "sin leading to death" in 1 John 5:16. Is there a point where a person can become so enmeshed in sin that we should stop praying for him?
   _____
   _____
   _____

Psalm 73—A Parallel Study

As much as we may disagree with the position of the atheist and fear for his eternal soul, often we see the short-term success he enjoys—often, seemingly, because of the distance between himself and godliness—and we are jealous. We don't understand why God seems to be treating His detractor so much better than His own people. And, frankly, we resent it.

As it is the fool who denies God, so also it is the fool who becomes embittered against God in such times (Psalm 73:21-22). But it is an unthinking animal that assumes God must be accountable to him and not vice versa.

The "glory" (v.24) awaiting us later is far better than anything we are denied in this life. The "good" (v.28) coming from being in the presence of God, both then and now, is far better than anything the world offers, and it motivates us to inform the fool of the folly of his way, and the blessings that come from acknowledging what God does for us.

1. Can we come to think our efforts toward holiness are "for nothing" (v.13)? How do we keep from growing bitter in our faithfulness? _____
   _____
   _____

2. In what sense does it betray God's people (v.15) to openly discuss atheism? __
   _____
   _____
   _____

3. Put Psalm 73:26 in your own words. _____
   _____
   _____
   _____

4. What is your favorite line in the psalm? Why? _____
   _____
   _____
   _____

The Faithless: A Case Study

"Ethan's just going through a phase." That's what Ethan's parents said when he was 14. He went through another "phase" at 16. And his 18-year-old "phase" was one for the books.

After years of posing "hypothetical" questions about basic spiritual issues in Bible class, Ethan had finally found in his college professors people who would give him different answers than he had been getting—answers, finally, that "made sense."

Case File

Ethan
• 18 years old
• College freshman
• Doubting the existence of God

Matthew, the local preacher fully expected Ethan to avoid church services when he came back home for the Christmas holidays. But he came. And he came ready to argue. The arguments flew—far faster than the preacher could properly respond, which was fine with Ethan, given that he wasn't really interested in hearing the responses anyway.

"The age of the earth proves the historical record in the Bible to be inaccurate."

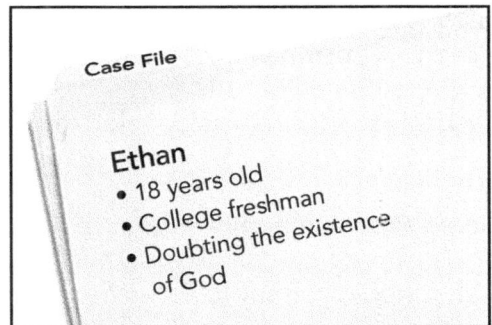

"Darwinian evolution is a proven fact. The Bible is out of touch with science."

"The existence of God is unproven and unprovable, and the pursuit of an answer is interfering with finding solutions to real world problems."

"The Bible is just another old book. It was written by men, just like any other old book. And just like any other old book, it has some good points and some not-so-good points. But the idea of thinking it comes directly from God is insanity. Everyone knows it is chock-full of contradictions, prejudicial judgments, misogynistic rants, cultural oddities, and fairy tales. No intelligent person would think otherwise."

"Heaven is a dream world made up by people dissatisfied with their lot in life and not empowered enough to change it. By filling people's heads with heaven nonsense, we are giving them false hope—and we are giving ourselves an excuse for not being proactive enough in coming to their aid here and now."

"Religion has caused more division, more wars, more bloodshed than any other branch of human philosophy in history."

"Anyone who thinks people like him are the only ones with the answers is arrogant to the point of grandiosity." (That one struck Matthew as highly ironic.)

"If you are interested in an actual discussion about these matters," Matthew said, after trying vainly to rebut a few of his fast-flying allegations, "I would be glad to sit down with you and deal with your issues point by point."

"Absolutely," Ethan said. "I look forward to it." Of course, he never did.

Read Psalm 14 again—this time with Ethan in mind.

What would you say to Ethan based on Psalm 14? _____
_____
_____
_____

New Testament Insight

All have turned away; all alike have become corrupt.
There is no one who does good, not even one.
— Psalm 14:3

Psalm 14 distinguishes between David's actions as a follower of God and the actions of the godless. The corruption of the world is a direct result of its failure to acknowledge and serve God.

In Romans 3:9-18, Paul makes a much more literal interpretation of David's words. Although true when referring to rebellious mankind, all of mankind is rebellious in the fullest, purest sense of the word—"For all have sinned and fall short of the glory of God" (Romans 3:23).

Paul quotes from Psalm 14 and several other passages, mostly from the Psalms, to emphasize the need for a Savior for all of mankind, not just the "really wicked" ones. Not one of us can claim that we have never acted as though there were no God. Not one of us is truly wise as God defines wise.

The terror that awaits the godless awaits us as well if we depart from our faithfulness. But "if we walk in the light as He Himself is in the light" (1 John 1:7), we can have confidence that, despite our failings, He will deal with us in mercy and compassion instead of the justice we deserve. Although we still are not "good" (Luke 18:19), by His grace we don't have to be.

The Faithless: A Hymn Study

Aaron W. Dicus vowed at his baptism in 1908, at the age of 20, that if God would grant him a good education, he would use that education to His glory. He spent the next 70 years doing just that.

Dicus used the education God blessed him with to become a physicist, inventing the automobile turn signal along the way. While chairing the physics department at Tennessee Tech, he trained several students who went on to work on the Manhattan Project. Later he served as professor at Florida College; his reputation in the scientific community was instrumental in getting accreditation for the school. Through it all, he continued to preach the gospel faithfully. He also served as a congregational overseer.

When *TIME Magazine* famously asked in its April 8, 1966 cover article, "Is God Dead?," Dicus felt compelled to answer. Already going blind from glaucoma and cataracts in his retirement years, he had seen enough of God's creation to weigh in mightily on the question. He staunchly defended the existence of the Creator, the One who "holds the germ within His hand." The human quest for answers, based on the scientific method he had learned so well, was inherently flawed, he argued in song—"for God alone does understand."

Dr. Dicus died in Tampa, Florida, on September 2, 1978. Of the more than 35 hymns he penned in his career, his two anthems of faith written in an era of doubt—"Our God, He Is Alive" and "Lord, I Believe"—remain by far his most popular.

Our God, He Is Alive

1. There is, be-yond the az-ure blue, A God con-cealed from hu-man sight;
2. There was, a long, long time a-go, A God whose voice the proph-ets heard;
3. Se - cure is life from mor-tal mind; God holds the germ with-in His hand,
4. Our God, whose Son up-on a tree A life was will-ing there to give,

He tint-ed skies with heav'n-ly hue And framed the worlds with His great might.
He is the God that we should know, Who speaks from His in-spired word.
Tho' men may search, they can-not find, For God a-lone does un-der-stand.
That He from sin might set man free And ev - er-more with Him could live.

There is a God (there is a God); He is a-live (He is a-live);

In Him we live (in Him we live) and we sur-vive (and we sur-vive),

From dust our God (from dust our God) cre-at-ed man (cre-at-ed man);

He is our God (He is our God), the great I AM (the great I AM).

Words: Aaron W. Dicus
Music: Aaron W. Dicus
© 1966 Aaron W. Dicus, assigned 1973 Sacred Selections, Inc.

Db - 4 - SOL

The Faithless: A Worship Study

A violent thunderstorm had kept many of our regulars home, but the ones who braved the elements were all glad they did. We had a spirited and uplifting discussion on evidences, capped by the singing of "Our God, He is Alive." The blasts of thunder and lightning were not distracting; indeed, they seemed to punctuate the powerful message we were sharing with one another regarding the power and majesty of the God we serve.

I noticed Ashlynn duck out toward the bathroom during the last stanza of the song. She did not come back for a few minutes, so Tracie and I tracked her down. We found her in a back bedroom, quietly crying.

"That song always reminds me of Eric," she said, referring to her ex-husband. "I always thought he was the strong one, the one who kept me from straying off course. And then—well, you know. He comes home six months ago, after three years of marriage, and says he's leaving me, that he's found someone else." (The "someone else" was another man—a fact that, as usual, went unspoken.)

"And when I talked to him about what the Bible said about marriage, about the life he was choosing, he said he had been faking it for years, that he wasn't sure he ever really believed the Bible, and that he certainly didn't believe in a God who would deny him his happiness."

"Did it shake your faith?" Tracie asked.

"I think it did, more than I probably let on. But every time we would sing that song, I kept thinking, 'My faith isn't in Eric. It's in God. And despite the questions I may have and the problems that arise, God is God. He's 'beyond the azure blue,' and sometimes that seems a million miles away. But he's there.'"

What does "Our God, He is Alive" mean to you? _____

_____

_____

_____

The Bible Study Song list

If you were putting a list together for a study about faithlessness, what songs would you include? Why? _____

_____

_____

_____

What songs might you exclude? Why? _____

_____

_____

_____

Psalm 16
A Song for the Hopeful

Good circumstances come and go. Fortunes wax and wane. For Christians, as we put our ultimate faith in God, the current climate is almost irrelevant. It is our future to which we look, not our present. And since our future is everlasting and glorious, we will not be overly thrilled or discouraged by what may come on any given day.

The Israelites inherited family parcels of land when they occupied Canaan under Joshua's leadership. Which tribe and which family would receive what land was determined "by lot" (Joshua 14:1-5). This is not exactly the same as "by chance," since we presume God controlled the process when lots were used for sacred purposes—"The lot is cast into the lap, but its every decision is from the LORD" (Proverbs 16:33). But the process does have the appearance of randomness. And as a result, resentment toward the "lucky ones" often ensues.

David knew his real future is with God, not his possessions. Being able to say, "You hold my future" helped him say, regardless of the details, "The boundary lines have fallen for me in pleasant places; indeed, I have a beautiful inheritance." It may be that he received a productive tract of land through God's grace; more likely, he is taking joy in his true inheritance, his relationship with his God. And that "inheritance" could not be more pleasant.

The Holman Christian Standard Bible renders verse 10, "For You will not abandon me to Sheol; You will not allow Your Faithful One to see the Pit." Capitalizing "Faithful One"

1 Protect me, God, for I take refuge in you.
2 I said to the LORD, "You are my Lord;
I have no good besides You."
3 As for the holy people who are in the land,
they are the noble ones in whom is all my delight.
4 The sorrows of those who take another god
for themselves multiply;
I will not pour out their drink offerings of blood,
and I will not speak their names with my lips.
5 LORD, You are my portion and my cup of blessing;
You hold my future.
6 The boundary lines have fallen for me in pleasant places;
indeed I have a beautiful inheritance.
7 I will praise the LORD who counsels me—
even at night my conscience instructs me.

8 I keep the LORD in mind always.
Because He is at my right hand, I will not be shaken.
9 Therefore my heart is glad, and my spirit rejoices;
my body also rests securely.
10 For You will not abandon me to Sheol;
You will not allow Your Faithful One to see the Pit.
11 You reveal the path of life to me;
in Your presence is abundant joy;
in Your right hand are eternal pleasures.

is in keeping with the sermon Peter delivers in Acts 2, attaching Jesus' resurrection to this prophecy. However, leaving "me" lowercase earlier in the verse gives the impression that David referred first only to himself and then only to the Messiah, which seems unlikely. And the use here of the term "the Pit" gives the impression that the one dying (whether Jesus or David) was not buried at all, which clearly was not the case. Most other versions use "corruption" or "decay," which, along with the idea of a soul "abandoned" to Sheol, better allows for an application to Jesus, who did die but did not remain entombed.

The verse works very well both as an assurance to us and as a prophecy of the Lord's resurrection. David certainly had the confidence that God would protect him from harm and death—not only conceptually but also literally, assuming David had not yet been given the throne of Israel as God had promised. Inspiration assures us that the deeper meaning, Jesus' conquest of the grave, is also at least part of the picture. The two-level hope in David's heart can be ours as well. Because of the marvelous way he saw God taking care of him in this life, David had the utmost confidence that He would continue to do so even after life on earth had passed. In the same way, we also can entrust ourselves to a faithful God as Jesus did (1 Peter 2:23), knowing that His resurrection gives us confidence of our own (1 Corinthians 15:12-20).

1. The psalmist refuses to have spiritual fellowship with "those who take another god" (v.4). Explain how we can apply that concept practically today. _____
_____
_____
_____
_____
_____

Portion

Figure of Speech

When God told Aaron that he and the rest of the priests would not receive a land grant in Canaan, He told him, "I am your portion and your inheritance among the Israelites" (Numbers 18:20). The ability to come before Him and serve in His temple was inheritance enough. So should it be with us.

Jokes abound as to whose "mansion" will be bigger in heaven. Such jesting demeans the glory awaiting all the faithful. Even if God were to reward some more than others in eternity, none of us would be cheated. None will receive less than he deserves; all will receive far, far more. Whatever God wishes to grace us with in heaven will be portion enough to give Him all the praise for all of eternity.

In the wreckage of Jerusalem, Jeremiah wrote, "The LORD is my portion, therefore I will put my hope in Him" (Lamentations 3:24). Being comfortable in life is nothing; being with God in heaven is everything.

2. Find a passage where Jesus offers His commentary on the word "good." Describe how His definition fits in with the psalmist's thoughts in verse 2. __
   _____
   _____
   _____

3. How does God "reveal the path of life"? What is that path? _____
   _____
   _____
   _____

4. What is your favorite line in the psalm? Why? _____
   _____
   _____
   _____

The Hopeful: A Bible Study

Paul says the Christian has "one hope" (Ephesians 4:4). Of course, we hope for many things throughout our lives, and many of those hopes are of a spiritual nature. But the hope of heaven surpasses all others by far. It is not a hope of desperation or of last resort; no, our hope comes with a real expectation. We do not hope for heaven because we are unsure; we hope for heaven because we are absolutely sure.

This confident expectation is seen in Paul himself as he anticipates his own death in the not-too-distant future. He writes, "In the future, there is reserved for me the crown of righteousness, which the Lord the righteous Judge, will give me on that day, and not only to me, but to all those who have loved His appearing" (2 Timothy 4:8).

The confidence he has been placing in Jesus throughout the years is precisely what emboldens him to anticipate heaven. Later in the same context he catalogs some of the hardships he has faced. Through it all, no matter who deserted or disappointed him, Jesus never did. Because of that, he writes in verse 18, "The Lord will rescue me from every evil work and will bring me safely into His heavenly kingdom. To Him be the glory forever and ever! Amen." It is interesting that the "evil work" to which he refers does not seem to be that of the Jews who trumped up charges to get him arrested initially, nor to the Romans who ultimately would take his life. No, the "evil" he remembers at the end was the betrayal of close, trusted brethren. Surely nothing can be a bigger discouragement or temptation to quit than that. Yet, as was the case with countless trials in times past, the Lord gave him the strength to endure.

Paul told the Colossians that God had already made them partakers in "the kingdom of the Son He loves" (Colossians 1:13). But the blessings we have as prospective residents of heaven are nothing compared to what awaits us. Truly, "our citizenship is in heaven, from which we also eagerly wait for a Savior, the Lord Jesus Christ. He will transform the body of our humble condition into the likeness of His glorious body, by the power that enables Him to subject everything to Himself" (Philippians 3:20-21).

That is our hope. May it be realized quickly.

Read Psalm 16 again—this time with Paul in mind.

1. In what sense is the kingdom of God here today? In what sense is it futuristic?
   _____
   _____
   _____

2. For what do the people of the world "hope?" What does it say about us when we find ourselves hoping for the same things? _____
   _____
   _____
   _____

Psalm 71—A Parallel Study

When we find ourselves closer to the end than the beginning, it is natural to look back on the life that has been lived and perhaps re-evaluate whether that path will be the right one for the remaining years. The psalmist writes, "I have leaned on You from birth; You took me from my mother's womb" (v.6). But was that the right decision?

The answer is an emphatic yes. "But I will hope continually and will praise You more and more," he writes in verse 14. As he affirms his commitment to God, he urges God to do the same for him. This and many other prayers in the Bible should not be taken to mean God will be far from the man or woman of faith if he or she fails to ask. Rather, it is yet another example of us being asked to pray for the things of which God has already assured us. Such prayers remind us of how much God has helped us in the past, and how committed He remains to us.

1. What are some other examples of things God promises us, yet asks us to pray for anyway? Cite Scripture. _____

   _____

   _____

2. Do the references to instruments in verse 22 indicate anything with regard to the possible use of instruments in worship today? Why or why not? _____

   _____

   _____

   _____

3. Read verses 10-14 again. Does the faithful one wait until there are signs of improvement before he begins to celebrate his victory? _____

   _____

   _____

   _____

4. What is your favorite line in the psalm? Why? _____

   _____

   _____

   _____

The Hopeful: A Case Study

Patricia was the only one in the hospital room without a tear in her eye. Her four children, thirteen grandchildren and three great-grandchildren, as well as innumerable friends, took turns coming in to boost her spirits, only to find that they were the ones whose spirits really needed boosting. And as always, Patricia was the woman for the job.

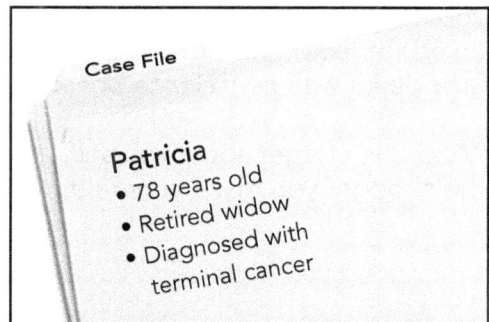

Case File

Patricia
- 78 years old
- Retired widow
- Diagnosed with terminal cancer

"It's all right," she kept saying. "I've had a great life. But it's enough. It's time to go."

"Are you sure?" asked her oldest, Tina, yet again, with tears streaming down her face.

"Sweetie, I've never been more sure in my life. If I was concerned about you and the boys"—even with her sons in their 50s, she still called them "the boys"—"maybe I would hesitate more. But you are all doing great. Your husband is an elder now. You've raised a bunch of wonderful kids. I couldn't be more proud."

"Do you have any fear" Tina asked. "I mean, really?"

Patricia paused for a moment. "No, I don't think so. I'm curious. Very curious. I've been getting ready for this moment for a long, long time. Now, if I didn't have my faith, if I hadn't spent my life serving the Lord, I can see why someone would be afraid. Even if they didn't believe in hell, I mean. The unknown is a scary thing." Then she smiled. "But not this unknown."

"What do you mean, Mom?"

"I mean this 'unknown' isn't completely unknown. I know I'm going to see your dad. I know I'm going to see my parents. Best of all, I know I'm going to see the Lord. Whatever the rest of it looks like doesn't matter."

"But do you really know? I have to admit, Mom, sometimes I have doubts."

"Of course you do, sweetie. We all have those moments. But for me, ever since your dad died, I've been trying to think a little bit about heaven every day. I talk about heaven in all of my prayers. And I think the more heaven is on my mind, the more real it gets."

"I'll miss you, Mom."

"I know, sweetie. But we'll be together again soon. Just think about me and your father, tell your grandkids to tell their grandkids about us—about how we loved the Lord, about how we lived in faith, and about how we were able to face death with confidence because of it.

"And don't forget about yourself, either. Keep building your faith. I promise you, the stronger you make your faith, the stronger you will find your hope to be."

Read Psalm 16 again—this time with Patricia in mind.

What would you say to Patricia based on Psalm 16? _____

_____

_____

_____

New Testament Insight

You will not abandon me to Sheol;
You will not allow Your Faithful One
to see the Pit.   — Psalm 16:10

Several passages referring to blessings promised to the faithful of God are ful-filled, in far greater fashion, in the person of Jesus. Such is the case with Psalm 16:8-11. Surely we all can have confidence that God will protect us and guard us from harm. But this is figurative language. It is not intended to tell us that godly men and women will not be allowed to die; in fact, we know that just the opposite is true.

The principle is literally true for Jesus. "Sheol" or "the Pit" means more than simply the grave a dead body inhabits, or even the realm of the dead where souls go to await judgment. In the Psalms, Sheol is a place of dread, a place to be avoided at all cost, a place from which there is no return. It is closer in meaning to death itself than to a particular gravesite on this plane or a particular abode in the spiritual plane.

Jesus did die, literally. He did inhabit the grave, literally. But His death was not like ours. He died knowing full well that He would rise again (Matthew 16:21). There was no fear in death for Him.

As obscure and difficult a distinction as this may be to us, Peter seems to have thought it was within the grasp of his readers to have seen it coming (Acts 2:24-32). Thankfully we have inspiration to reveal to us what we likely never would have fully comprehended on our own.

The Hopeful: A Hymn Study

The Great Chicago Fire of 1871 destroyed the business and fortune of Horatio Spafford. The financial panic of 1873 made things worse. Unable to take his family to Europe as planned, he sent them ahead on the *S.S. Ville du Havre*. The ship collided with another vessel and sank, taking the lives of his four daughters. Sailing to meet with his wife, who survived, Spafford penned his most famous words near the very spot his daughters lost their lives.

It Is Well with My Soul

1. When peace, like a riv - er, at - tend - eth my way,
2. Though Sa - tan should buf - fet, though tri - als should come,
3. My sin— O the bliss of this glo - ri - ous tho't!—
4. And, Lord, haste the day when the faith shall be sight,

When sor - rows like sea bil - lows roll,
Let this blest as - sur - ance con - trol,
My sin, not in part but the whole,
The clouds be rolled back as a scroll;

What - ev - er my lot, Thou hast taught me to say,
That Christ hath re - gard - ed my help - less es - tate
Is nailed to the cross, and I bear it no more.
The trump shall re - sound, and the Lord shall de - scend—

"It is well, it is well, with my soul."
And hath shed His own blood for my soul.
Praise the Lord, praise the Lord, O my soul!
E - ven so, it is well with my soul.

CHORUS

It is well (It is well) with my soul (with my soul),

It is well, it is well, with my soul.

Words: Horatio Spafford
Music: Philip P. Bliss

D♭ - 4 - SOL

The Spaffords' trials were not over. After losing a son to scarlet fever at the age of 4, the Spaffords were regarded by the Presbyterian church as smitten of God. Spafford took his wife and two young daughters, born after the sh pwreck, to Jerusalem, where they founded the American Colony. Their group assisted the needy of all faiths. It provided essential relief in the ravages of World War I, running soup kitchens, hospitals and other charitable works. Swedish novelist Selma Lagerlöf wrote her Nobel Prize-winning book *Jerusalem* about the American Colony.

Philip Bliss was one of the greatest and most prolific hymn writers and composers of the 19th Century, although he only wrote hymns in the last dozen years of his life. He wrote the music to "It Is Well with My Soul" and introduced it at a meeting of ministers in November 1876 in Chicago. A month later, on December 29, 1876, he and his wife were on a train bound for Ashtabula, Ohio, when a bridge collapsed and sent the train carriages into a ravine. Bliss survived but went back into the burning wreckage to save his wife. Neither was seen again. The Blisses left behind two sons, ages 4 and 1.

The Hopeful: A Worship Study

After the study one Saturday night, several of us went to the hospital to visit Patience. At only 34 years old, she was going into surgery the next Monday to remove a tumor the size of a golf ball from her brain.

Any fears we might have had about putting a damper on a fine evening were quickly dashed. She was wide awake and attentive, playing cards with her husband, Mitch. He seemed far more frazzled than she; I couldn't help thinking she was keeping his spirits up and not the other way around.

They quickly put the cards away and let us know about the procedure (intimidating) and the prognosis (uncertain). When she remembered it was our study night (she and Mitch were regulars), she asked what song we had been focusing on. She lit up when she heard the title of one of her favorites. "Sing it for me, please?" We didn't have our music, but we had no trouble singing four stanzas from memory. We unconsciously kept the volume down a bit (it was a hospital, after all), but Patience quickly starting jerking her thumbs upward. "Louder, louder," she mouthed. We complied. By the time we sang the last note, half the staff and several patients had gathered outside to listen.

"I think about that song a lot these days," Patricia said afterward. "I had no problems seeing the good in life on my graduation day, or when I got my first job, or my wedding day." She looked over at Mitch and squeezed his hand. "So I think it's only fair that I get a chance to show my hope in God in some bad days now."

"Fair?" someone exclaimed. "You're so young!"

"How many days am I entitled to? Threescore and ten? Fourscore? How many does God owe me?"

"Your life is but a vapor,…" I said quietly.

"That's right. So I'm waking up Monday believing that it is going to be the best day of my life. And no matter how things go, I'll be right."

What does "It is Well with My Soul" mean to you? _____
_____
_____
_____

The Bible Study Song List

If you were putting a list together for a study about hope, what songs would you include? Why? _____
_____
_____

What songs might you exclude? Why? _____
_____
_____

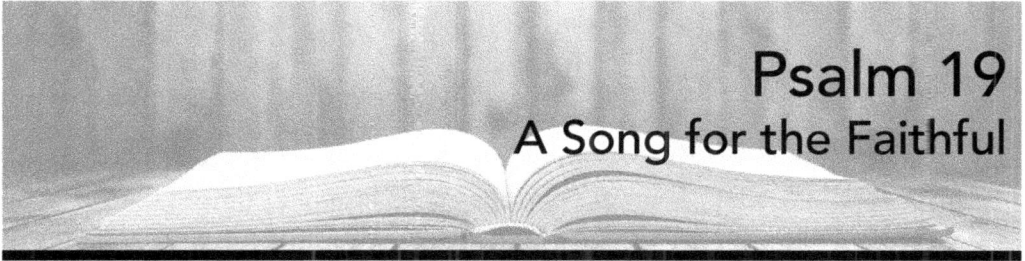

Psalm 19
A Song for the Faithful

God has left two great evidences of His existence, His power, and His love and care. Both are on full display in Psalm 19.

The unspoken testimony of the creation, being the first testimony ever given, appears first. The magnificent creation, particularly the sky and the celestial bodies, demand we recognize a Mind greater than all of these things. Although all aspects of God's creation speak to His power and excellence, the infinite expanse above us particularly impress upon us the certainty of a Divine Being who could put such a massive undertaking into such precise order.

God does not "speak" to us through the creation in the most literal of senses. He does not communicate specific information. This testimony is of the more general sort—not the requirements such a God might have of us, but rather His greatness, our smallness, and our need to seek out whatever requirements might exist.

This communication, though, however vague it might be, is more than sufficient to the task. Paul writes in Romans 1:18-20, "For God's wrath is revealed from heaven against all godlessness and unrighteousness of people who by their unrighteousness suppress the truth, since what can be known about God is evident among them, because God has shown it to them. From the creation of the world His invisible attributes, that is, His eternal power and divine nature, have been clearly seen, being understood through what He has made." Virtually every human who has ever lived

[1] The heavens declare the glory of God,
and the sky proclaims the work of His hands.
[2] Day after day they pour out speech;
night after night they communicate knowledge.
[3] There is no speech; there are no words;
their voice is not heard.
[4] Their message has gone out to all the earth,
and their words to the ends of the inhabited world.
In the heavens He has pitched a tent for the sun.
[5] It is like a groom coming from the bridal chamber;
it rejoices like an athlete running a course.
[6] It rises from one end of the heavens
and circles to the other end; nothing is hidden from its heat.

[7] The instruction of the LORD is perfect,
reviving the soul;
The testimony of the LORD is trustworthy,
making the inexperienced wise.
[8] The precepts of the LORD are right,
making the heart glad.
The commandment of the LORD is radiant,
making the eyes light up.
[10] All my enemies will be ashamed and shake with terror;
they will turn back and suddenly be disgraced.

has seen the sun rise and traverse the sky and been moved to acknowledge the existence of God—however uninformed their concept of "God" may have been. God wishes to make Himself known to all of mankind. He has done exactly that, in a way that cannot possibly escape the notice of any one of us.

General information as to the existence of God is not enough; that is why He condemns the Gentiles for corrupting the notion of the true God and serving idols. The more specific information about God's nature and His requirements for us are also praised in Psalm 19. The "perfect… trustworthy…pure…reliable" words of God, revealed through His prophets and preserved through the ages through His providence, are the greatest treasure He could give us in this life. They show us our shortcomings, instruct us as to how to improve, give us hope that the process is worthwhile, and produce in us a greatness of our own that reflects, however imperfectly, our Heavenly Father.

Since He has given us words of instruction, we are moved to give the words of our mouth to praise Him. We have been given the opportunity to know God, to serve Him, and to give Him thanks. And every day that we spend under His sun should be spent studying His word in dogged pursuit of those things.

1. What specifically about staring into the sky (day or night) causes you to reflect on the glory of God? _____
   _____
   _____
   _____
   _____
   _____
   _____
   _____

Figure of Speech

Honey

In an era where not only refined sugar but even a multitude of artificial sweeteners are abundant and easy to acquire, we may have trouble understanding the effect that honey had on the ancient world. Honey blessed the land and its inhabitants like no other substance.

Honey was understood in the day to be an important source of nutrition. It stands as a representation of the agricultural viability of the land; Canaan was valued because it was "flowing" with honey (Exodus 3:8). John the Baptist subsisted largely on it (Matthew 3:4). It gave Jonathan needed energy in time of physical depletion (1 Samuel 14:27). Nutritionists now know it serves as a source of antioxidants and necessary minerals such as iron and manganese.

God's word is not only sweet to the taste in the short term. It is a sign of God's eternal provision for us. Best of all, we can't get sick from eating too much, as is the case with literal honey (Proverbs 25:27).

2. Read verse 3 in a variety of versions. What is the main point the psalmist is trying to convey? _____
_____
_____
_____

3. What are our "hidden faults" and how does reading God's word help us find them and fix them? _____
_____
_____
_____

4. What is your favorite line in the psalm? Why? _____
_____
_____
_____

The Faithful: A Bible Study

We expect God to keep His promises. We do not apologize for that. He is the Faithful One; He is called that numerous times in the text (Deuteronomy 7:9; 1 Corinthians 1:9; 2 Timothy 2:13, Hebrews 10:23, etc.). He can be trusted to remain true to His nature. "So those who suffer according to God's will should, in doing good, entrust themselves to a faithful Creator" (1 Peter 4:19).

So why does it seem, from time to time, He has forgotten us? Our punishment is prolonged? Our forgiveness is delayed? Our oppressors prosper rather than suffer the punishment God promises to them?

We may never fully comprehend the answer. But Daniel gives us a good model for the child of God who understands what God has promised but not yet delivered. Daniel, prophesying in the first year of Darius (Daniel 9:1-2), knew the 70-year punishment given to Judah (see Jeremiah 25:11-12) should be coming to an end. Instead of asking God to keep up His end of the bargain, Daniel acknowledges God's righteousness in sending the punishment in the first place. He, like Nehemiah in his prayer (Nehemiah 1:4-11), emphasizes the unworthiness of the people—and includes himself, surely one of the more "righteous" ones in man's eyes, among those who have transgressed.

Daniel did not see himself as being more worthy of blessing from God than his predecessors, or indeed being worthy of anything at all. He took the opportunity to confess his own shortcomings, as well as those of his nation, and ask for God's continued patience and mercy. Then and only then, with a proper perspective, was Daniel in the right frame of mind to make a request from the God who had already given so much.

The 70 years of waiting are turned into yet another prophecy through Daniel. God tells him that the nation would be asked again to wait for deliverance—not from political oppression this time, but from sin; not by a foreign dictator, but by the King of kings, "Messiah the Prince" (Daniel 9:25). The 70 weeks—generally assumed to refer to "weeks" of years, 490 of them in total—are in a highly apocalyptic section of text; attempts to specifically identify the "years" in question are likely to result in a great deal of frustration. In any case, this misses the main point. Daniel is told that a time is coming when Messiah would "seal up vision and prophecy and...anoint the most holy place" (v.24), indicating that the true temple of God, the church (2 Corinthians 6:16), would appear, signifying a time in which piecemeal revelation of God's mind and will would end (1 Corinthians 13:9-12).

Read Psalm 19 again—this time with Daniel in mind.

1. Explain the timing of Judah's return. Did it happen under Darius or Cyrus (2 Chronicles 26:22-23)? Was Darius the son of Esther's Ahasuerus? _____
_____
_____

2. What does it say about us when we are willing to confess our sins? Use 1 John 1 to argue your point. _____
_____
_____

Psalm 118—A Parallel Study

The way of the child of God is not an easy one. But in all circumstances—before, after, and during hardship—he or she can find strength and motivation to "give thanks to the LORD." In fact, the existence of hardships only provides that much more for which we can be thankful; if deliverance has not yet arrived with regard to the current difficulty, we can be grateful for similar circumstances in which God saw us through; that will motivate us to give thanks for the help that He has not yet given but will surely arrive in His time and His way.

It is appropriate that the psalm is "bookended" by the same phrase: "Give thanks to the LORD, for He is good; His faithful love endures forever." At the beginning of our trials and through them all until the end, His love and care for us remains assured.

1. Find other occurrences in the Psalms of the phrase or its equivalent: "The LORD is for me; I will not be afraid. What can man do to me?" Explain its meaning.

   _____

   _____

   _____

2. Does verse 17 assure our difficulties will pass without harming us overmuch? Explain your answer. _____

   _____

   _____

   _____

3. Verses 22-23 are Messianic references. Is there another in Psalm 118? _____

   _____

   _____

   _____

4. What is your favorite line in the psalm? Why? _____

   _____

   _____

   _____

The Faithful: A Case Study

Donte' had been homeschooled by loving Christian parents. They had taught him to fear God and believe the Bible, but to think for himself. He had earned a scholarship to a good college, and he was planning to pursue a career in petroleum geology.

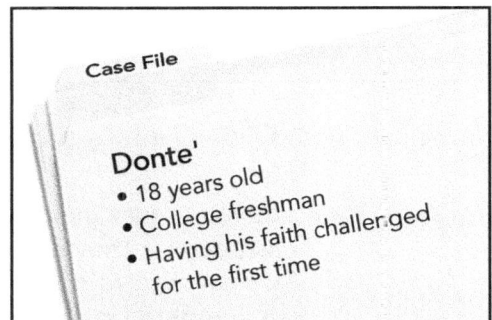

Case File

Donte'
- 18 years old
- College freshman
- Having his faith challenged for the first time

He knew the subject of creation vs. evolution would come up quickly in his science classes, and he was prepared. He spent much of the summer before his freshman year boning up on the arguments atheists make to debunk the Bible. He was ready for his faith to be assaulted, and, he had to admit, a small part of him was looking forward to a real confrontation.

Donte' felt incredibly small in the huge auditorium that held 300 other freshmen, trying to survive their first geology class. There was very little class participation, so Donte' decided to let the occasional reference to the ancient earth and the evolutionary timeline go without saying anything. Eventually, though, the professor made a comment about "backward anti-science types" who took God's word over scientific proof. Donte' raised his hand, but the professor did not call on him.

After class, Donte' approached the professor. Taking a deep breath, he said, "Sir, I'm a Christian. And I'm not anti-science. I certainly don't think I'm backward. I believe true science and true faith are compatible."

"Son," the professor interrupted, "I'm not going to have this discussion with you. If you want to believe in God, that's your business. Everyone has a right to be wrong. But I guarantee you, if you don't open up your mind to what your elders and betters are telling you, there is no way you will graduate with a degree from this department."

"I thought college was all about exposing yourself to all sorts of different points of view. That's what I'm trying to do. For instance, did you know there are more than 100 reliable dating methods that say the earth is less than 10,000 years old?"

"I told you, I'm not going to have this conversation," said the professor, irritated now. "And I would strongly advise you, young man, to learn how to go along and get along. I guarantee you, most of the staff in this department will not be as kind and patient with you as I have been."

Read Psalm 19 again—this time with Donte' in mind.

What would you say to Donte' based on Psalm 19? _____

_____

_____

_____

New Testament Insight

The stone that the builders rejected
has become the cornerstone.
This came from the LORD;
it is wonderful in our eyes.   — Psalm 118:22-23

The ultimate reward of the faithful was to be the arrival of Messiah, the fulfillment of the promises made to Abraham, Isaac and Jacob. Many of the references to the coming of Messiah are couched in contexts that do not appear immediately to be Messianic. Hebrew scholars believed the entirety of the Law, the Psalms and the Prophets provided bits and pieces to the puzzle, leading up to the time when Messiah would be fully revealed and the prophecies put in their proper perspective.

The "stone" in Psalm 118:22 is part of the picture of God coming to the relief of His beleaguered people; the source of relief would be rejected by those who should have known best, but God would bring about His salvation anyway. Jesus quotes the passage in Matthew 21:42 and the parallel accounts in Mark 12:10-11 and Luke 20:17. All three are given in the context of the parable of the vineyard owner whose slaves refused to give honor to the owner, even killing his son. The message was that Jesus would ultimately be successful in building His kingdom—but it would be despite the "experts," not because of them.

The text is also quoted in Acts 4:11, Ephesians 2:20 and 1 Peter 2:7, making it one of the most frequently referenced passages in the Old Testament.

The Faithful: A Hymn Study

Joseph Addison is considered one of the greatest writers in the history of the English language. He is best known for his writings in *The Spectator.* In the issue of August 23, 1712, he introduced an essay on strengthening faith in the heart of man with the following:

> The Supreme Being has made the best arguments
> for his own existence in the formation of the heav-
> ens and the earth, and these are arguments which
> a man of sense cannot forbear attending to who is
> out of the noise and hurry of human affairs…The
> Psalmist has very beautiful strokes of poetry to this
> purpose in that exalted strain (Psalm xix). As such
> a bold and sublime manner of Thinking furnished
> out very noble Matter for an Ode, the Reader may
> see it wrought into the following one.

He concluded the piece with what now stands as the lyrics to "The Spacious Firmament on High."

Franz Joseph Haydn, the Austrian composer, friend of Mozart and teacher of Beethoven, contributed the music that accompanies the hymn. Although it is common for writers in centuries past to have co-opted tunes from classical pieces to accompany sacred verses, in this case the lyrics far predated the music.

The Spacious Firmament on High

1. The spa-cious fir-ma-ment on high, With all the blue e-the-real sky,
2. Soon as the eve-ning shades pre-vail, The moon takes up the won-drous tale,
3. What tho' in sol-emn si-lence all Move round the dark ter-res-trial ball?

And span-gled heav'ns, a shin-ing frame Their great O-rig-i-nal pro-claim.
And night-ly to the lis-t'ning earth Re-peats the sto-ry of her birth;
What tho' no re-al voice nor sound A-mid the ra-diant orbs be found?

Th'un-wea-ried sun, from day to day, Does his Cre-a-tor's pow'r dis-play,
While all the stars that round her burn And all the plan-ets in their turn
In rea-son's ear they all re-joice, And ut-ter forth a glo-rious voice,

And pub-lish-es to eve-ry land The work of an al-might-y hand.
Con-firm the tid-ings as they roll And spread the truth from pole to pole.
For-ev-er sing-ing as they shine, "The hand that made us is di-vine."

Words: Joseph Addison
Music: Franz J. Haydn

Bb - 2 - SOL

The melody is adapted from Haydn's oratorio *The Creation*, the composer's own tribute to the Biblical creation story and widely considered his masterpiece. The last performance of *The Creation* Haydn attended was on March 27, 1808, about a year before he died. When the crowd arose to honor "Papa" Haydn, then weak and sickly at the age of 76, he pointed upward and said, "Not from me—everything comes from up there!"

The Faithful: A Worship Study

The weather could not have been better. The sky was cloudless, the air was crisp, the temperature was moderate. Having checked the forecast and seen the good news ahead of us, we decided to have the study in the afternoon out of doors instead of inside during the evening hours. Derek and Bridget, our hosts for the day, had to turn the porch lights on and bring out the flashlights so we could sing "The Spacious Firmament on High," a song that is complicated to sing even if you know it well (and many of us did not).

After the study, as was our custom, we ate pot-luck style—except this time Bridget had made enough barbecue to feed an army. The stars were coming out by the time we finished. The teenagers tried to play football in the growing darkness, the mothers went inside to check on the young children and make sure they were not destroying Bridget's house, and the men silently pulled up lawn chairs on the deck and stared up into the sky. It was a perfect day, one we did not want to end.

Derek broke the silence. "'In reason's ear they all rejoice/And utter forth a glorious voice,/Forever singing as they shine,/"The hand that made us is divine."' Do you think that's true?"

"Does creation speak to the ear of the one who is trying to 'reason' his way through life?" I asked. "Yes, I think so."

He shook his head. "I wish 'reason' would listen better," he said.

I nodded, and as one we all stared back at the stars, now growing in number and brightness, remaining silent for what seemed like half an hour. Finally, Derek said aloud what I think we all were thinking:

"It's tough to believe some people can't hear that."

What does "The Spacious Firmament on High" mean to you? _____
_____
_____
_____

The Bible Study Song List

If you were putting a list together for a study about faith, what songs would you include? Why? _____

_____

_____

What songs might you exclude? Why? _____

_____

_____

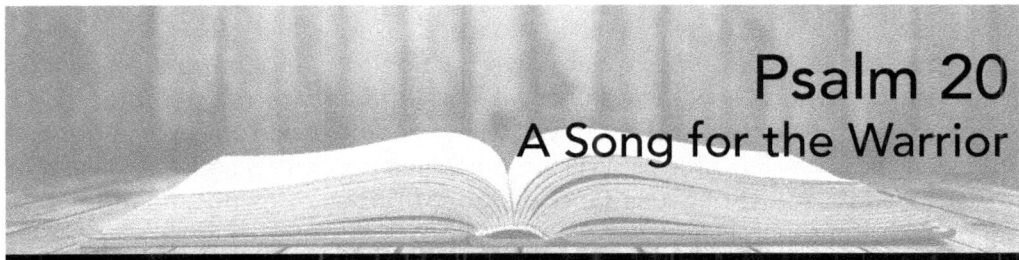

Psalm 20
A Song for the Warrior

Most of us have an emergency contact—a person who can be summoned at short notice to come to render aid. We choose the person carefully. There's no point in having an emergency contact who is unreliable, or who rarely is near the telephone, or who has poor transportation. We call the person who can help, who wants to help, and whose help will be what is needed at the time.

Emergencies come in life. When they do, we call God. The blessing placed upon the reader in verse 1, "May the LORD answer you in a day of trouble," should not be read so as to cast some doubt as to His ability to answer. Rather, it is a reminder to be the kind of people who know where true assistance can always be found. By "true assistance," the Christian always means aid rendered to the spirit. As difficult as life on earth is (and as willing as God is to render aid in carnal things), the true "emergency" in life is always found in our battle with "the spiritual forces of evil" (Ephesians 6:12).

Spiritual conflict is inevitable. Will we survive? Will we prosper? Will we conquer? The Christian has an advantage in these areas over others; he knows the war between good and evil will be resolved one day in favor of good—the side he has chosen.

He knows the conflict will end well because God is on his side. God cannot be defeated in any endeavor—certainly not the quest for the salvation of souls, a

¹ May the LORD answer you in a day of trouble;
may the name of Jacob's God protect you.
² May He send you help from the sanctuary
and sustain you from Zion.
³ May He remember all your offerings
and accept your burnt offering.
　　Selah
⁴ May He give you what your heart desires
and fulfill your whole purpose.
⁵ Let us shout for joy at your victory
and lift the banner in the name of our God.
May the LORD fulfill all your requests.
⁶ Now I know that the LORD gives victory to His anointed;
He will answer him from His holy heaven
with mighty victories from His right hand.
⁷ Some take pride in a chariot, and others in horses,
but we will take pride in the name of the LORD our God.
⁸ They collapse and fall,
but we rise and stand firm.
⁹ LORD, give victory to the king!
May He answer us on the day that we call.

cause that He took so seriously as to give His Son to die for it. So the question is not nearly so much how the conflict will go in the long term but rather how it will go in the short term—and not how it will go for the cause of Christ in general but rather how it will go for us. Will we ourselves be dealt a setback? Will that setback be fatal? Just because God will be victorious does not mean that we will be victorious with Him.

This is why the child of God is so determined to keep God on his side. He constantly petitions Him for help. He acknowledges his shortcomings and begs God to forgive.

Because we know the outcome beforehand, we can ask for help (v.4) and celebrate victory (v.5) simultaneously. The more we lean on God, the more we are reminded of His saving power, His willingness to come to our aid, and the superiority of His might.

The natural inclination is to put our confidence in the accomplishments and talents we imagine ourselves to have acquired without God's help—seen depicted in verse 7 as a chariot or a horse. The images of chariots and horses should show us the futility of trusting in ourselves. A king entering battle with thousands of chariots in times past might have appeared invincible; today, he would be dispatched by the most meager of modern armies in moments.

Circumstances change. Tactics change. But God does not change, nor should our confidence in Him. So having God on our side should be the only issue — not numerical strength, not the "advantages" gained by those who do not fight by God's rules, and certainly not any obligation on our part to be "strong enough" or "skilled enough" to carry the day.

God will win the victory; to Him be the glory.

1. What is it that our heart desires in verse 4? Is this authorization to ask God for absolutely anything and to have confidence we will receive it? Why or why not? _____
   _____
   _____
   _____

2. Twice in the psalm help is described as coming directly from the presence of God. What form might that help take? _____
   _____
   _____
   _____

Figure of Speech

Anointed

People called to a special task in times of old were anointed with olive oil. Psalm 133:2 describes the anointing of the first high priest, saying the oil was "running down Aaron's beard, on his robes." Samuel anointed both Saul and David as king.

"The anointed one" carries special authority for a special task. Appropriately, then, Jesus should be known to us as the Christ (or Messiah in Hebrew, meaning, "the anointed one"). Most translations use the phrase "His Anointed One" in Psalm 2:2, a clear Messianic text. Jesus, and only Jesus, could put into effect the divine plan for the salvation of sinful humanity.

We also, as Christians, are singled out. We read in 1 John 2:20, "But you have an anointing from the Holy One, and you all have knowledge." This may have some reference to gifts of the Holy Spirit, but in a broader sense it means Christians have been singled out by the Spirit as the only ones who may be "built into a spiritual house for a holy priesthood to offer spiritual sacrifices acceptable to God" (1 Peter 2:5).

3. How might we show that we "take pride in the name of the LORD our God?"

_____

_____

_____

_____

4. What is your favorite line in the psalm? Why? _____

_____

_____

_____

The Warrior: A Bible Study

Occasionally we find an example of someone standing for the Lord with such aggression and disregard for convention that we think to ourselves, "Surely this has gone too far." And invariably we find instead that God applauds "extreme" efforts in His cause, that no degree of commitment to the Lord is "too much."

One of the best examples of this is Phineas, the grandson of Aaron and the future high priest of Israel, as told in Numbers 25. When the prophet Balaam failed to curse Israel at the behest of Balak, the king of Moab, the women of Moab brought the wrath of God upon Israel by enticing them sexually and encouraging them to worship idols. God responded by sending a plague that took the lives of 24,000 Israelites.

In the throes of the plague, one Israelite man has the audacity to parade a Midianite woman before his family and the nation. Although the Midianites were not as notoriously idolatrous as the other tribes Israel encountered (Moses married a Midianite), this union seems to have fallen under the same condemnation as did the associations with the Moabites. (Numbers 25:16-17 alludes to another incident, not recorded in the text, when the Midianite king attempted a similar attack on the morality of the nation.) And Phinehas, caught up in extreme religious fervor, followed the two of them into their tent and stabbed them both through with a single spear thrust.

Phinehas' ancestor, Levi, was noted for his lack of control over his temper (Genesis 34:25, 49:5-7). Even Moses and Aaron struggled with anger (Numbers 20:6-11). But Phinehas' rage was rooted in holiness and a love for God's word, not selfishness, spite or arrogance. As a result, God reacts to Phinehas' outburst far differently than the others; He credits the zeal of Phinehas alone for staying His righteous anger, which threatened to destroy the entire nation (Numbers 25:12). No one is suggesting that we go around impaling adulterers today. But the degree of hatred against sin seen in this story should give us pause the next time we give tacit approval to illicit sexual activity or blasphemy. God takes such things very seriously.

Read Psalm 20 again—this time with Phinehas in mind.

1. Does the sinful behavior of one member of the body of Christ have an impact on the whole? What should be done in such cases? Does the nature of the sin in question matter? _____
   _____
   _____
   _____

2. Were there 24,000 adulterers and idol worshipers in the camp of Israel on that day? Is it possible that some died as a consequence of the sins of others? What implications does that have for us in the church? _____
   _____
   _____
   _____

Psalm 124—A Parallel Study

Psalm 124 is remarkable for the number of metaphors used in such a short space to describe the onslaught vented toward the people of God by their enemies.

Verse 3 describes the attackers potentially swallowing God's people alive "in their burning anger"; death by drowning in a violent storm is described in verses 4-5. Being rent asunder by their teeth and being trapped like a bird in a net follow in verses 6-7.

Through it all, God was with His people. Disaster would definitely have struck, the psalmist asserts, "If the LORD had not been on our side." He is the One who tears the net, allowing us to escape. He is the One who stills the storm. Since He is "the Maker of heaven and earth" (v.8), it is not surprising that He is able to come to the defense of those who love and serve Him, mustering His entire arsenal of weapons and tactics. Therefore it is pointless, and faithless, to see only the hardships of life in His service without seeing the ultimate deliverance that waits for us on the other side.

1. How do we know for sure that God is on our side? Are there any visible, outward signs of His approva ? _____
   _____
   _____
   _____

2. What sort of opposition do ycu face in your daily and weekly walk with Christ?
   _____
   _____
   _____
   _____

3. Describe the opposition you may have heard of regarding Christiars today, perhaps in other parts of the world. What can we say to such ones in their time of difficulty? _____
   _____
   _____
   _____

4. What is your favorite line in the psalm? Why? _____
   _____
   _____
   _____

New Testament Insight

LORD, give victory to the king!
May He answer us on the day that we call.
— Psalm 20:9

The one who is lost must first acknowledge that he is lost. Then he acknowledges God as the only One through whom salvation can come. Then he expresses his faith in God and responds to His invitation of grace. This, in a nutshell, is calling on the name of the Lord.

It is incumbent upon the lost soul to reach out to his Savior. God will not involuntarily save anyone. "Now without faith it is impossible to please God, for the one who draws near to Him must believe that He exists and rewards those who seek Him" (Hebrews 11:6). Such has been the case for all time.

Prophecy indicates a special way in which the people of God would call upon Him in the Messianic era. Joel 2:28-32 indicates specific signs—"signs from heaven" as they were called in Jesus' day (Matthew 16:1-4)—that would signify the dawn of a new age. "Then everyone who calls on the name of Yahweh will be saved, for there will be an escape for those on Mount Zion and in Jerusalem, as the LORD promised, among the survivors the LORD calls."

Peter in Acts 2:21 and Paul in Romans 10:13 quote Joel 2:32 and apply it to the gospel time. It is through believing the gospel of Jesus Christ that people can come to a true knowledge of God's will for mankind. Thus, anyone "calling on His name" in obedient faith, as Paul did (Acts 22:16) will be saved.

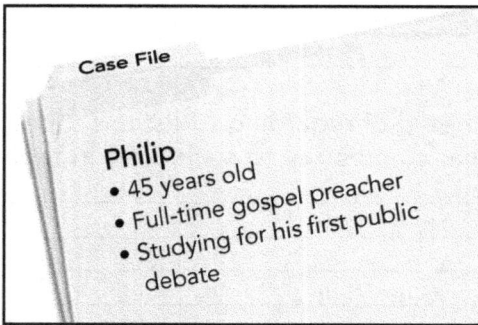

The Warrior: A Case Study

Case File

Philip
- 45 years old
- Full-time gospel preacher
- Studying for his first public debate

Philip was prepping for a debate—his first. He had developed a bit of a rapport over the years with his opponent, who preached for a large denominational group in town. This would be their most intense and broad-based discussion by far.

He was getting a great deal of advice, much of which seemed contradictory. His moderator, an old-school debater himself, encouraged him to be aggressive. "Take every opportunity to make a distinction between your position and his," he said. "Don't be rude, but don't be afraid to help a silly point of his look sillier. Don't chase his rabbits. He will do whatever he can to distract you from your point. Stay focused. Talk about what you are prepared to talk about. Don't show weakness or doubt. Don't concede anything."

Philip's wife, who was not exactly excited when Philip told her about the debate plans, was concerned that the argumentative, combative tone being encouraged by the moderator would do more harm than good in the long run. "You still have to live in the same town as this man," she pointed out. "You will see his parishioners all the time at the barbershop or the Olive Garden. You don't want them to remember you as some jerk who wouldn't let their man get a word in edgewise. Make your point, certainly. But don't get personal. Keep smiling. Don't talk about hell or who might go there.

The church elders were supportive but concerned that weaker members might be discouraged if the debate were to get too deep. "This is your show, Philip," Brother Mason said. "We are not going to tell you how to do your job other than to be true to the word—the same as with your preaching. But I think I speak for us all when I say we would like you to try to avoid making the truth sound too complicated. Personally, I'm not too impressed by scholarly arguments anyway. And if we give people the impression that we need a bunch of special training and college like you have, we might discourage them from thinking they will ever be able to read the Bible for themselves."

Philip felt dizzy.

"Lord, I need help," he found himself praying. "I don't know which way to go. I want to know the truth. I want to stand on it firmly. I want to share it with others, as plainly and completely as I can. I want to treat my fellow man with dignity and respect. I want to train my brethren in how to walk in Your way. And certainly, I want souls to be saved.

"I don't know how to pursue all of those things at the same time. But You ask Your children to put themselves in Your hands in the day of trouble. And that is what I am doing today.

"Please help me.

"Amen."

Read Psalm 20 again—this time with Philip in mind.

What would you say to Philip based on Psalm 20? _____
_____
_____
_____

The Warrior: A Hymn Study

Charles Wesley and his brother, John, are credited for forming what became the Methodism movement in the 18th century. The Wesleys and their followers were heavily persecuted in their native England. No doubt the real oppression they faced informed the classic hymn Charles Wesley wrote depicting the spiritual

Soldiers of Christ, Arise

1. Sol - diers of Christ, a - rise And put your ar - mor on,
2. Strong in the Lord of hosts, And in His might - y pow'r;
3. Stand then in His great might, With all His strength en - dued,
4. Leave no un - guard - ed place, No weak-ness of the soul;
5. That, hav - ing all things done And all your con - flicts passed,

1. Sol - diers of Christ, a - rise

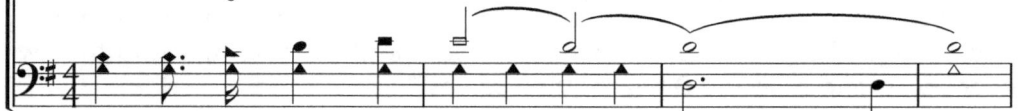

1. Sol - diers of Christ, a - rise And put your ar - mor on,

Strong in the strength which God sup - plies,
Who in the strength of Je - sus trusts
But take, to arm you for the fight,
Take eve - ry vir - tue, eve - ry grace,
You may o'er - come thru Christ a - lone,

Strong in the strength which God sup - plies,

Strong in the strength which God sup - plies Thru His be - lov - ed Son.
Who in the strength of Je - sus trusts Is more than con - quer - or.
But take, to arm you for the fight, The pan - o - ply of God;
Take eve - ry vir - tue, eve - ry grace, And for - ti - fy the whole;
You may o'er - come thru Christ a - lone And stand en - tire at last.

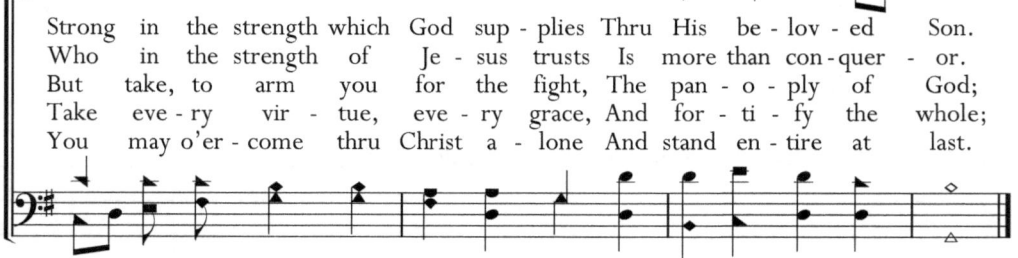

Words: Charles Wesley
Music: Bradbury's *Jubilee*

G - 4 - DO

battle Christians wage against Satan that is so vividly depicted in the well-known "armor of God" passage, Ephesians 6:10-17.

Written in 1747 and originally entitled, "The Whole Armour of God, Ephesians VI," the hymn had twelve verses of eight lines apiece. Several of the rhyming couplets were cobbled together over the years to form the five verses we have in most of our hymnals.

One of the now-omitted stanzas refers to the shield of faith being made of "adamant and gold." This seems to be a reference to John Milton's classic work, *Paradise Lost*, in which the devil wages war against God "armed in adamant and gold," It is thought Wesley envisioned the Christian army turning Satan's weapons against him.

The hymn has been sung over the years to several tunes, including an original of Wesley's and "Diademata" by Sir George Job Elvey; it may be more familiar to us as the tune to "Crown Him with Many Crowns." The tune in most or all of our hymnals is by William Bradbury, one of the great hymn composers of the 19th Century. Bradbury's compositions include the tunes for "Just as I Am," "Tis Midnight and on Olive's Brow," "The Solid Rock," and "Jesus Loves Me."

The Warrior: A Worship Study

"Does it strike anyone else as odd that we seem incapable of singing songs like 'Soldiers of Christ, Arise!' while sitting down?" I asked after we sang the classic hymn—standing, naturally.

I was not really expecting a substantive response. But I got one anyway.

"I'll tell you what has always struck me as odd," Phoebe said. "We sing the song standing up because the song tells us to stand up. So we arise. We sing the song. Hopefully, with help from the worship leader, we sing it with vigor and heart. And then what do we do?"

A lengthy pause ensued. Finally someone said, "We sit down, I guess." And everyone chuckled.

"That's right," Phoebe continued. "We sit down. And we go about our business as though nothing happened. Nothing changes."

"Well, I sort of want everybody to sit down at that point," I add, half-joking. "Usually it's time for me to start preaching." ("Then by all means, let's remain standing!" some wiseacre chimed in, drawing laughs from all.)

"But seriously," Phoebe persisted, "doesn't that speak to the whole concept of the song service? We're not trying to motivate ourselves for the next five minutes or half-hour. We're already motivated to that degree. What we need to do is go home with this song still ringing in our ears. We need to 'arise' at the office, 'arise' at school, 'arise' at home. Always be prepared to fight the devil, because we know he is always going to be prepared to fight us."

What does "Soldiers of Christ, Arise!" mean to you? _____

_____

_____

_____

The Bible Study Song List

If you were putting a list together for a study about warriors, what songs would you include? Why? _____

_____

_____

What songs might you exclude? Why? _____

_____

_____

Psalm 23
A Song for the Shepherd

For a herding culture like Israel, the image of shepherding resonated well. Everyone understood about sheep. Their inability to care for themselves. Their propensity for trouble. Their stubbornness. But also, in a positive vein, their willingness to be led, and their tremendous capacity for providing blessings in the form of wool, milk, offspring and manure.

The key is the shepherd. Having a shepherd who truly cared for the sheep, who put their welfare above his own, makes the difference between a productive and growing flock and a rebellious, unkempt and scattered flock. Of course, even the best of shepherds will have poor sheep, and the best efforts to discipline them may fail; a good shepherd will know when to cut his losses with a sheep that spreads disease and discontentment.

The analogy is spot-on with regard to God's relations with His people. We, too, are naturally helpless in the face of life's difficulties—and yet stubborn in our insistence that we know what is best for us. We get into trouble often, and we try to get others into trouble with us. Through it all, we have tremendous capacity for good. And God sees that, and works with us to help us achieve a level of service far beyond anything we might have managed on our own. But we have to listen to the Shepherd.

It has been observed that Psalm 23 effectively takes us through an entire year for the sheep in the care of the shepherd. In the springtime, he takes them out of the paddock and leads them to where they will find good grazing areas to eat and then lie down to ruminate. Since sheep tend to get spooked around running water, the shepherd finds smooth pools and calm streams so the sheep can

¹ The LORD is my shepherd; there is nothing I lack.
² He lets me lie down in green pastures;
He leads me beside quiet waters.
³ He renews my life;
He leads me along the right paths
for His name's sake.
⁴ Even when I go through the darkest valley,
I fear no danger,
for You are with me;
Your rod and Your staff—
they comfort me.
⁵ You prepare a table before me
in the presence of my enemies;
You anoint my head with oil;
my cup overflows.
⁶ Only goodness and faithful love will pursue me
all the days of my life,
and I will dwell in the house of the LORD
as long as I live.

drink in peace. If the sheep finds itself stuck in a gully, a bush, or even turned upside-down and unable to right itself, the shepherd restores order. Later in the grazing season, when the weather gets warmer and drier, he will lead them up into the plateaus where they will stay for weeks at a time. The mountain passes that must be traversed are treacherous, but the sheep will go through the most dangerous of them if the shepherd is with them.

The sheep finds nothing but "goodness and faithful love" as long as it submits to the shepherd. So also we, as the sheep of Jesus' fold (John 10:11-15), are blessed beyond measure in His care.

1. What is it that we "want" for in this life? How is it that God will supply it? __
_____
_____
_____
_____

2. Can a sheep ever get to a point where it cannot be restored? Can we? Explain.
_____
_____
_____
_____

3. What do God's "rod and staff" represent? How do they give us comfort? ___
_____
_____
_____
_____

4. What is your favorite line in the psalm? Why? _____
_____
_____
_____

The Shepherd: A Bible Study

If we are ever of a mind that an elder candidate must have a spotless record, we need only think of Peter. Peter's love and enthusiasm for the Lord were unparalleled in times of comfort and fellowship. But we all know the story of how adversity struck from an unexpected direction and Peter was caused to say he did not even know who Jesus was (Luke 22:54-62). The gaze Jesus cast across the high priest's courtyard at Peter must have been a look Peter never forgot.

Peter learned from his mistake. Just as he denied the Lord three times to strangers in front of a charcoal fire that fateful morning, so also Jesus gave him three

Overflowing Cup

Figure of Speech

The importance of a cup lies in what is or will be inside. In the extreme, the "cup" can refer to the actual contents, as was the case with the cup that Jesus "shared" or "divided" at the Last Supper but clearly remained physically intact (Luke 22:17-20, Mark 14:23-24); the "cup" surely refers to the fruit of the vine.

God's blessings are too great to be contained in any "cup" we may have. The people are encouraged to test God's limits in Malachi 3:10—"See if I will not open the floodgates of heaven and pour out a blessing for you without measure." Joel uses the image for both God's blessings for His people and His wrath against His enemies (Joel 2:24, 3:13).

In return, we are asked to "overflow" in bestowing blessings upon others. In 2 Corinthians 8:2, the Macedonians were so full of joy in Jesus Christ that it "overflowed into the wealth of their generosity," manifesting in their contribution to the needy Jerusalem saints.

chances to affirm his loyalty. And by the Galileean lake, on another morning, in front of another charcoal fire, Peter passed the test. All three of them.

Perhaps it was Peter's future work as an elder to which Jesus referred on that occasion when, after Peter's threefold affirmation of love and commitment, He said, "Feed My lambs...Shepherd My sheep...Feed My sheep" (John 21:15-17). His point seems to be that merely professing love for the Master was not enough—that testimony must be given. Another generation would arise that would need more from Peter than he had been prepared to offer on that fateful day; it would be his responsibility to minister to the people of God as Jesus had ministered to him. Judging from Peter's strong testimony and affirmation of apostolic authority in 2 Peter 1:16-21, we can safely assume he made the Lord proud.

Peter's closing words of inspiration serve as guidance for all who would be guided by the Chief Shepherd (1 Peter 5:4) and by His inspired leaders who carried His word to the world. "Therefore, dear friends, since you have been forewarned, be on your guard, so that you are not led astray by the error of the immoral and fall from your own stability. But grow in the grace and knowledge of our Lord and Savior Jesus Christ. To Him be the glory both now and to the day of eternity. Amen" (2 Peter 3:17-18).

Read Psalm 23 again—this time with Peter in mind.

1. Do Peter's words in the Bible carry equal weight with Jesus'? Explain your answer. _____
_____
_____

2. How might Peter's failures in following Jesus' guidance have helped when souls under his direct care went astray? _____
_____
_____
_____

Psalm 78—A Parallel Study

It is fitting that Psalm 78 begins with the psalmist impressing upon the nation the necessity of teaching a new generation about the ways of God. He then proceeds to do just that, reminding them of the constant care God had shown His people over the generations, only to have His generosity thrown back in His face. They refused to learn the lessons of their forefathers.

Finally, victory is obtained. Judah is elevated over Ephraim (v.67-68)—looking not only back to the blessing given the patriarch Judah over his brethren in Genesis 49:8-10, but also forward to the future, in which Judah (the Southern Kingdom) would be preserved and Ephraim (the Northern Kingdom) lost. Likewise the "David" mentioned in verse 70 refers not only to the unifying king of the past but also the ultimate King who would come to reign over His people in the future.

1. How can we act as "shepherds" for the next generation? Cite Biblical examples of those who did and those who did not. _____
_____
_____

2. What characterized God's "shepherding" of Israel over the generations? __
_____
_____
_____

3. Jeremiah 30:9, Ezekeil 34:23-24 and Ezekiel 37:24-25 use the name David to refer to the Messiah. What similarities do we see between David and Christ? Is Psalms 78:70 another Messianic reference or just a look back at the literal David? _____
_____
_____
_____

4. What is your favorite line in the psalm? Why? _____

_____

_____

_____

The Shepherd: A Case Study

The elders had approached Patrick, one of the deacons, about possibly receiving an appointment as elder himself. Like most candidates, especially the really good ones, Patrick was hesitant. He had tremendous respect for the existing elders and had trouble seeing himself on a spiritual par with them. So he visited the local preacher, Joseph, and asked for his advice.

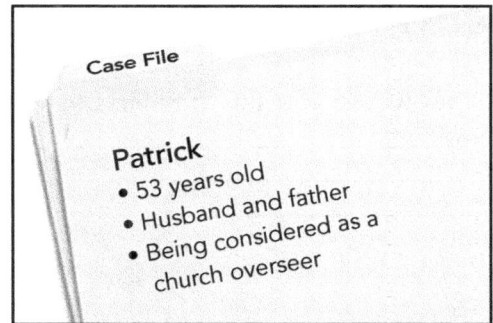

Case File

Patrick
- 53 years old
- Husband and father
- Being considered as a church overseer

The two men read aloud from 1 Timothy 3 and Titus 1, detailing the character of a man who is to serve as a congregational overseer. "Do you see anything in this description that does not look like you?" Joseph asked.

"I'm a bit concerned about having my children under control," said Patrick, the father of four of the best young Christians Joseph had ever been around. "Jason is only 14, and I am starting to think we might have more trouble with him than with the others."

"Jason is a fine young man," Joseph insisted. "And you have two off on their own already, blessing the church where they are. And Erika is a fine young woman who does you proud every day. We're hoping desperately she decides to stay home for college; we need her in the teaching program." Patrick smiled at the praise despite himself.

"I suppose it's just the enormity of it all. I take Hebrews 13:17 very seriously. The thought of answering for the souls of others is a little terrifying, I have to admit."

"No reasonable man would think otherwise," Joseph countered. "But it's not like God expects you to drag everyone in the directory through heaven's gates personally. He is just going to expect you to do your best. And I've never known you to offer less."

"I'm worried our relationship with the church members will change."

"Oh, it will change, I guarantee that. And not necessarily for the better. People chafe at leadership. You'll learn all new ways for your brethren to let you down. You'll learn things you never wanted to know. "

"Well, you've just about convinced me," said Patrick with his usual splash of irony.

"They call it *serving* as an elder for a reason," Joseph said. "It's work to put others first. But as far as I can tell, you're not considering this position because it will help your social standing. You're considering it because you are a servant of the church. And you know in your heart this is the best way you can serve."

Read Psalm 23 again—this time with Patrick in mind.

What would you say to Philip based on Psalm 23? _____
_____
_____
_____

New Testament Insight

> The LORD is my shepherd;
> There is nothing I lack.   — Psalm 23:1

If "shepherds" provide oversight for local congregations, it should not surprise us to find that Jesus Himself is the "Chief Shepherd" for the entire church. Peter assigns Him this role in 1 Peter 5:4. The "judgment calls" among the people of God in a particular location are determined by the local shepherds. But the doctrinal guidance is always provided by the Lord.

So if Psalm 23 is a depiction of our heavenly Father's care for His children, so also Jesus fits the description. He provides us with spiritual nutrition (John 6:35). He gives us living water to drink in abundance (John 4:14). He takes souls lost in sin and sets them aright again, "raised with Him through faith in the working of God" (Colossians 2:12). He shows us the path in which we are to walk (1 John 1:7) by walking in it Himself while in the flesh (1 Peter 2:21-22). He gives us hope when we stare death in the face by giving us confidence of emerging victorious on the other side (1 Corinthians 15:20-22), and the discipline that He endured in His own body emboldens us to prosper under His rod and staff (Hebrews 12:3-13). And surely "goodness and faithful love will pursue" the one who commits himself to the One who is goodness and love personified.

The Shepherd: A Hymn Study

A young preacher named Joseph Gilmore was to deliver a sermon on March 26, 1862. He had been assigned the subject Psalm 23, a text he had handled several times before. But this time he was captivated by the phrase, "He leadeth me." He wrote later, "Those words took hold of me as they had never done before, and I saw them in a significance and wondrous beauty of which I had never dreamed." Later, while conversing about the sermon, he wrote the lines that have come to be known so well, handed them to his wife, and thought no more about it. Unbeknownst to him, she sent it to *The Watchman and Reflector*, which published it.

He Leadeth Me

1. He lead-eth me, O bless-ed thought! O words with heav'n-ly com-fort fraught!
2. Some-times mid scenes of deep-est gloom, Some-times where E-den's bow-ers bloom,
3. Lord, I would place my hand in Thine, Nor ev-er mur-mur or re-pine,
4. And when my task on earth is done, When by Thy grace the vic-t'ry's won,

What-e'er I do, wher-e'er I be Still 'tis God's hand that lead-eth me.
By wa-ters still, o'er trou-bled sea, Still 'tis His hand that lead-eth me.
Con-tent, what-ev-er lot I see, Since 'tis my God that lead-eth me.
E'en death's cold wave I will not flee, Since God through Jor-dan lead-eth me.

He lead-eth me, He lead-eth me, By His own hand He lead-eth me;

His faith-ful fol-l'wer I would be, For by His hand He lead-eth me.

Words: Joseph H. Gilmore
Music: William B. Bradbury

D - 4 - SOL

Well-known hymn composer William Bradbury, who was well known for discovering talented hymn writers (including, most notably, Fanny Crosby), ran across "He Leadeth Me," set it to music, added a chorus, and published it in one of his hymnals.

Three years after he wrote the hymn, Gilmore was in Rochester, N.Y. to preach for a church there and perhaps be taken on for the full-time work. He idly picked up a hymnal and opened it; much to his surprise, he saw his hymn there, "He

Leadeth Me." To that point he did not even know his poem from three years before had even been acknowledged, let alone made into a hymn for singing.

Joseph Gilmore, son of New Hampshire governor Joseph A. Gilmore, went on to become a college professor and the author of six books. Although Gilmore wrote several other hymns, none has had the long-term success and popularity of "He Leadeth Me."

The Shepherd: A Worship Study

I was surprised when Perry raised his hand after we sang "He Leadeth Me." Perry was a regular at the class, and he seemed to participate in the singing—although he did not lead. But he had not made a single comment in any of the class sessions. I called on him, and he took a moment to gather his thoughts before speaking. When he did finally speak, it was in a near-whisper.

"Maybe I'm off here," he said, "but whenever I sing 'He Leadeth Me,' I think about my dad. He didn't lead singing very often, but when he did, it was 'He Leadeth Me' as often as not. So as a kid I learned to cringe whenever he got up on singing night and said, 'Number four hundred and seven, please. Four-oh-seven.' I can hear him saying it now, clear as day."

Perry began to tear up a bit. "But ever since he died a few years ago, I've started to think of 'He Leadeth Me' as a song about parenting. I know that's not the main point. But I think to all the things Dad taught me over the years: How to drive, how to barbecue, how to treat my wife. And especially how to serve the Lord.

"So now, with my son, I try to be the kind of leader for him that my dad was for me. I want him to know that whatever he does, wherever he is, he will always have me there to help him, guide him, and love him."

What does "He Leadeth Me" mean to you? _____
_____
_____
_____

The Bible Study Song List

If you were putting a list together for a study about shepherds, what songs would you include? Why? _____
_____
_____

What songs might you exclude? Why? _____
_____
_____

Psalm 26
A Song for the Innocent

If a tree has integrity, it means the tree is solid all the way through. It is structurally sound, free of internal decay. What you see is what you get.

The same thing goes for a person with integrity. He not only puts on the appearance of being a certain way, he actually is that way at the core of his being. Usually we use the term to refer to someone who is pure. Having the appearance of innocence might be good enough for someone who simply wants to have a good reputation. But to the one who wants to please God, who knows us inside and out, nothing less than true innocence will do.

The one who is hypocritical fears having his innocence tested; he knows he will fail. But the one with integrity looks forward to the test. He is not embarrassed about what it will reveal. Not only has he been keeping his own thoughts and behaviors in the ways of God; he has even been avoiding those who think and act otherwise. Instead of their company, the innocent delights in "the house where You dwell, the place where Your glory resides" (v.7). The obvious application of this concept would be the temple—or the tabernacle, in the time of David. But the average person did not go into the tabernacle to commune with God; that was strictly for the priests. Certainly it could be said that the child of God goes to a place of worship to come in contact with God; we do that as Christians every Lord's Day, whether the "house" is an actual building (Acts 20:7-8) or not. The

[1] Vindicate me, LORD,
because I have lived with integrity
and have trusted in the LORD without wavering.
[2] Test me, LORD, and try me;
examine my heart and mind.
[3] For Your faithful love is before my eyes,
and I live by Your truth.
[4] I do not sit with the worthless
or associate with hypocrites.
[5] I hate a crowd of evildoers,
and I do not sit with the wicked.
[6] I wash my hands in innocence
and go around Your altar, LORD,
[7] raising my voice in thanksgiving
and telling about Your wonderful works.
[8] LORD, I love the house where You dwell,
the place where Your glory resides.
[9] Do not destroy me along with sinners,
or my life along with men of bloodshed
[10] in whose hands are evil schemes,
and whose right hands are filled with bribes.
[11] But I live with integrity;
redeem me and be gracious to me.
[12] My foot stands on level ground;
I will praise the LORD in the assemblies.

psalmist alludes to worship in the last verse of the psalm. But any "house," be it a physical structure or a person's family, used to honor God can be a place where His glory is seen. Certainly we look forward to the place in the Father's house that Jesus promised to prepare for us after we leave this life (John 14:2-3).

1. In what ways could association with evildoers impact the status of the innocent?
   _____
   _____
   _____
   _____

2. If dwelling in the Lord's house is truly our fondest desire, how will that desire manifest itself in day-to-day life on earth? _____
   _____
   _____
   _____

3. Do innocent people ever suffer for the wrongdoing of others? If so, does that mean that God is indifferent to the difference between innocent and guilty?
   _____
   _____
   _____
   _____

4. What is your favorite line in the psalm? Why? _____
   _____
   _____
   _____

The Innocent: A Bible Study

Since most of the book of Job describes Job's complaints to God about his condition (a less generous person might term it "whining"), and since we really hate listening to complainers, it is easy to miss the main point of the book, which is this: Job is innocent. He is being tested by Satan, and he passes. We have inspired Scripture telling us so (Job 1:22; 2:10).

Innocent people don't stop having problems when it is determined that they are innocent. Often, in fact, it makes their problems tougher for them to bear. Job does not fear scrutiny from the hand of God; in fact, he welcomes and solicits it. But the more silence from the throne of God regarding Job's culpability, the more frustrated Job gets.

Washing Hands

Figure of Speech

As is often the case, the Bible was ahead of its day with regard to scientific knowledge. We know today that washing your hands is an important part of regular hygiene. Water removes not only visible grime but also invisible germs and other impurities.

Washing was an important part of the cleanliness ritual for the priests under the Law of Moses (Exodus 30:17-21). Eventually it became symbolically attached to holiness and the removal of spiritual impurities. The religious leaders of Jesus' day were outraged that Jesus and His disciples would dare to eat without participating in the ceremonial washing (Luke 11:38; Matthew 15:2), elevating their tradition to the level of God's law.

Perhaps the most famous incident involving symbolic hand-washing is in Matthew 27:24; there Pontius Pilate, the man responsible for issuing a crucifixion order, washed his hands in front of the angry mob to demonstrate his own innocence (in his own mind, at least) of Jesus' righteous blood.

Job does not claim flawlessness; as with any person of character who understands about sin, he acknowledges that no one could possibly stand completely justified on his own merits before a holy God (Job 9:2-4). What he does credit himself with is blamelessness, or innocence. It astounds him that the same pattern of suffering would be given both to the blameless and the wicked, giving the impression that He is indifferent to it all (Job 9:21-24). He eagerly hopes for an opportunity to speak to God face to face and inquire as to why such things are happening to himself, a righteous man.

> If only I knew how to find Him,
> so that I could go to His throne.
> I would plead my case before Him
> and fill my mouth with arguments.
> I would learn how He would answer me;
> and understand what He would say to me.
> Would He prosecute me forcefully?
> No, He will certainly pay attention to me.
> There an upright man could reason with Him,
> and I would escape from my Judge forever. (Job 23:2-7)

The challenge with being innocent is maintaining one's humility. No, we may not "deserve" what we are receiving by any conventional rationale. Then again, we are not completely innocent; "For all have sinned and fall short of the glory of God" (Romans 3:23). And "the wages of sin is death" (Romans 6:23). By that reckoning, we are getting off easy. The one who maintains his humility in the midst of unfair adversity is the one who truly passes the test.

If we can maintain our hope in God as our caretaker and (ultimately) our defender (Job 13:15-16), we can manage to escape the hard and unjust treatment of this life with our faith intact. If we can take it a step further and find peace in our relationship with God, we will have a far easier time of it. As Job himself said, in a time when perhaps he did not realize how long and painful his trial would be, "Shall we accept only good from God and not adversity?" (Job 2:10).

Paul writes in Philippians 2:14-15, "Do everything without grumbling and arguing, so that you may be blameless and pure, children of God who are faultless in a crooked and perverted generation, among whom you shine like stars in the world." Anyone can suffer and complain about it. What makes the child of God special is his or her ability to suffer without cause and not complain about it. This is a whole other level of blamelessness. Job eventually gets there (Job 42:1-6). Hopefully it won't take us as long.

Read Psalm 26 again—this time with Job in mind.

1. What should we say to those who claim the hardships we are encountering are testimony to our unfaithfulness? _____
   _____
   _____
   _____

2. What effect did Job's friends have on his relationship with God and on his ability to deal with circumstances? What lessons can we draw for ourselves?
   _____
   _____
   _____

Psalm 101—A Parallel Study

If you ignored the first verse of Psalm 101, the rest could easily be understood to have been written in the voice of God. He honors integrity. He rejects godlessness. He destroys the slanderer. The reason these are the author's intentions is because they reflect the values given to Him by His creator, in whose image he is made.

As it is, it is written in David's voice—whether literally by his hand or not. And David's commitment to keep his palace and kingdom free (as much as he could manage, naturally) of evil is an excellent example for us as we exercise control over our small corner of God's world. His implementation of these values was far from perfect, as ours certainly will be. But having a high standard for ourselves and falling short from time to time is far better than having a low standard, or no standard at all.

1. Why do righteous people, with values similar to David's, embrace sin so frequently? Why did David? What can be done to prevent it happening to us? _____
   _____
   _____
   _____

2. How committed should we be to avoiding contact with sin? Cite relevant Scripture. _____
   _____
   _____
   _____

3. We are not in a position to "destroy anyone who secretly slanders his neighbor" as David was. How far should we go in opposition to the sin of our society?
   _____
   _____
   _____
   _____

4. What is your favorite line in the psalm? Why? _____
   _____
   _____
   _____

The Innocent: A Case Study

On Sunday, Bianca, one of the high school students in the congregation, asked to meet with Jared, the local preacher. Jared and his wife, Wendy, met with Bianca at the church building that afternoon. Bianca told them she had been sexually abused for years by her uncle, an elder in the church. Horrified, Jared pulled Bianca's father and uncle aside

Case File

Jared
• 43 years old
• Gospel preacher
• Caught between the alleged victim and the accuser

after the evening worship service. Emphasizing that he was not taking Bianca's story at face value, he laid it out before them. The father was furious; the uncle was humiliated, naturally, but maintained his innocence. Jared excused himself from the conversation as quickly as possible, offering his services as mediator if they should be required at all. He didn't sleep very well that night.

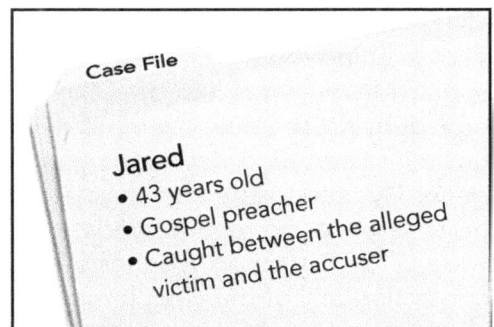

Monday morning, the uncle visited Jared at the church office. "I just wish you hadn't gotten involved in all this," he said.

"Trust me, it wasn't my idea," Jared emphasized. "She came to us. But when she did, what was I supposed to do? Maybe I should have brought her father into the discussion at the time, but it all happened so fast. I hardly had time to process it all."

"You should have brought me in, too."

"Well, I don't know how I could have done that, bringing the accused perpetrator in to confront the emotional (alleged) victim. But I did reach out to you as quickly as I could."

"So what do we do now? You do believe me, right?"

Jared hesitated. "I'm not sure it's right for me to make a liar out of either one of you right now. If you're asking whether I think you are a rapist, then no, I don't. But I don't think Bianca is a hysterical, self-centered attention hog who would make up a horrible story like this, either."

"If word gets out about this, I might be forced to step down as elder. You know that, right? That would dissolve the eldership, harm the church. I can't have that."

"The church will survive one way or the other," Jared assured him. "You just worry about putting things right in your family."

"Did you call the police?" he asked.

"No, of course not. Neither did Wendy. It's not our place. Whether your brother did or not, I don't know. I didn't ask."

That evening the elders called Jared back to the building and fired him on the spot. They accused him of making up the entire story (Bianca, evidently, was now denying she ever even met with Jared and Wendy), blackmailing Bianca's uncle into stepping down and getting Jared installed as elder in his place, and generally tearing the church apart for personal gain. He was given no notice, no severance, no recommendation. He was told whatever books or materials were still his office on Wednesday would be discarded. He was forbidden from contacting any of the church members, and from attending any services of the church beginning with the next Wednesday evening's Bible study. He was threatened with bodily harm if he had any contact whatsoever with Bianca, whether he initiated it or she did.

Early Tuesday morning, a brick went through Jared and Wendy's living room window. A profane note was wrapped around it.

Wednesday morning, Jared and Wendy's home of ten years had a "FOR SALE" sign in the front yard.

Read Psalm 26 again—this time with Jared in mind.

What would you say to Jared based on Psalm 26? _____
_____
_____
_____

New Testament Insight

> No one who acts deceitfully will live in my palace;
> no one who tells lies will remain in my presence.
> — Psalm 101:7

Since Psalm 101 is described as "Davidic," we can think of it being in David's voice, whether or not he was actually the one who composed the psalm. As the king, he had control over who would have access to him. He mentions several character flaws specifically, but he seems to emphasize honesty and integrity. He absolutely refuses to allow dishonest ones to share his close proximity.

Revelation 21:8 includes "all liars" among those who are denied access to "the Holy City, new Jerusalem"—who instead are doomed to suffer in "the lake that burns with fire and sulfur, which is the second death." In a society where lying is commonplace, and in which it is actually applauded under certain circumstances, we need to be reminded of the affront to holiness inherent in deception.

God Himself "cannot lie" (Titus 1:2). It is "impossible" for Him to do so (Hebrews 6:18). When Paul writes that God "cannot deny Himself" (2 Timothy 2:13), he means that God's holiness, faithfulness and truthfulness emanate from His nature—the nature we are trying to acquire for ourselves. If we are to behave as He behaves, with regard to truthfulness or any other area, we must learn to value what He values.

The Innocent: A Hymn Study

Frances Ridley Havergal, one of the most talented hymnists of the 19th Century, died on June 3, 1879, at the age of 42, having been plagued with poor health for much of her life. She claims to have been truly committed to God only for the last seven years of her life. In a relatively short time, though, she wrote dozens of popular hymns, many of which remain in common usage to this day. Aside from "Take My Life and Let It Be," her most popular ones today likely are "I

Take My Life and Let It Be

1. Take my life, and let it be Con-se-crat-ed, Lord, to Thee.
2. Take my hands, and let them move At the im-pulse of Thy love.
3. Take my voice, and let me sing Al-ways, on-ly, for my King.
4. Take my will, and make it Thine; It shall be no long-er mine.
5. Take my love, my Lord, I pour At Thy feet its treas-ure store.

Take my mo-ments and my days; Let them flow in cease-less praise.
Take my feet, and let them be Swift and beau-ti-ful for Thee.
Take my lips, and let them be Filled with mes-sag-es from Thee.
Take my heart, it is Thine own; It shall be Thy roy-al throne.
Take my-self, and I will be Ev-er, on-ly, all for Thee.

Words: Frances R. Havergal
Music: McIntosh and Cunningham's *New Life*, arr. Rigdon M. McIntosh

A - 3 - SOL

Gave My Life for Thee," "Truehearted, Wholehearted," "Is It for Me?" and "I Bring My Sins to Thee."

Havergal described the creation of "Take My Life and Let It Be" thusly:

> Perhaps you will be interested to know the origin of the consecration hymn, "Take my life." I went for a little visit of five days. There were ten persons in the house, some unconverted and long prayed for, some converted but not rejoicing Christians. He gave me the prayer, "Lord, give me all in this house!" And He just did! Before I left the house every one had got a blessing. The last night of my visit I was too happy to sleep, and passed most of the night in praise and renewal of my own consecration, and these little couplets formed themselves and chimed in my heart one after another, till they finished with, "Ever, ONLY, ALL for Thee!"

As the meter for the hymn is a common one, "Take My Life and Let It Be" has been paired with a wide variety of tunes through the years. "Yarborough" by

William B. Bradbury is the one familiar to most American Christians, although a derivative of a tune by Wolfgang Amadeus Mozart is also favored.

In the prelude to her 1870 collection, Ministry of Song, Havergal described her poetry:

> Amid the broken waters of our ever-restless thought,
> Oh be my verse an answering gleam from higher radiance caught;
> That where through dark o'erarching boughs of sorrow, doubt and sin,
> The glorious Star of Bethlehem upon the flood looks in,
> Its tiny trembling ray may bid some downcast vision turn
> To that enkindling Light, for which all earthly shadows yearn.
> Oh be my verse a hidden stream, which silently may flow
> Where drooping leaf and thirsty flower in lonely valleys grow;
> And often by its shady course to pilgrim hearts be brought,
> The quiet and refreshment of an upward-pointing thought;
> Till, blending with the broad bright stream of sanctified endeavor,
> God's glory be its ocean home, the end it seeketh ever.

The Innocent: A Worship Study

It was the first time in the class for the Johnstons, a family that was new to the area and the congregation. They came with their 4-year-old son, Judah, who decided he would rather sit outside with his mom and dad and the rest of the grown-ups than go into the back bedroom and watch Scooby-Doo cartoons with the other children, with whom he had not really bonded yet. Of course, we had no problem with that.

As it turned out, Judah was quite a singer. He didn't know all of the songs very well; we were spending time learning some new ones. But for whatever reason, he was really excited about singing "Take My Life and Let it Be." He belted out every stanza, just as loud and proud as anyone else.

Curious, I went up to the Johnstons afterward and complimented Judah on his singing. "I was wondering, Judah, did you like the last song we sang?" He nodded with a smile. "What did you like about it?" He just shrugged, still smiling. I was thinking I wouldn't get much of a response, but then Mr. Johnston pitched in to help.

"Judah, what do we give to Jesus?"

Grinning, Judah stretched his arms out as wide as they would go. "All for Dee! All for Dee!" he sang, just as loud as before.

"That's very good, Judah," I said. "So do you know what that means?"

"That means, when Jesus comes to my house to play, I will let Him play with all my toys, and watch all my movies, and play all my games."

"Wow! That is very nice of you, Jonah."

"Yes. But Jesus will let me play too. Except He gets to go first." Clearly this was a conversation he had had with his parents many times.

"That sounds great, Jonah. I think that is very nice of you to do that. I want to ask you something. When Jesus comes to play at your house, can I come too?"

He looked me hard in the eye, sizing me up. Then he smiled. "Yes, you can come. But you have to remember, Jesus goes first."

"I'll remember that, Judah. Jesus goes first."

What does "Take My Life and Let it Be" mean to you? _____
_____
_____
_____

The Bible Study Song List

If you were putting a list together for a study about innocence, what songs would you include? Why? _____
_____
_____

What songs might you exclude? Why? _____
_____
_____

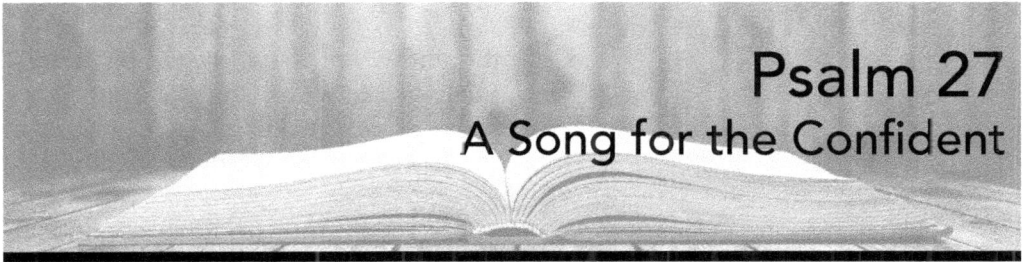

Psalm 27
A Song for the Confident

Fear is the great neutralizer. Fear of failure, fear of rejection, fear of retribution, fear of loss, fear of the future—we could go on and on. We believe in God. We hope in God. But we cannot manage to get that faith, such as it is, to manifest itself in our day-to-day confrontations with the opponents of Jesus Christ.

Truly, we should be praying along with the father of the spirit-possessed boy, "I do believe! Help my unbelief" (Mark 9:24).

A deep, abiding, "mountain-moving" faith looks adversity in the face and smiles—not because of his own ability, but because of the greatness of the God who stands with him. Truly, as Paul writes in Romans 8:31, "What then are we to say about these things? If God is for us, who is against us?" Paul doesn't suggest here that the enemies of God will run and hide from us when they realize what God we serve; rather, the point is that the identity and number of our opponents is irrelevant when we consider who our ally is.

For the truly confident Christian, the only thing more delightful than the opportunity of serving God in this life is enjoying fellowship with Him in the next. We do enjoy the privileges of serving in His temple, the church (2 Corinthians 6:16, 1 Peter 2:5) while here on the earth. But the greater "temple," the greater "house" awaits us. Just as David could speak convincingly and au-

[1] The LORD is my light and my salvation—
whom should I fear?
The LORD is the stronghold of my life—of
whom shall I be afraid?
[2] When evildoers came against me to
devour my flesh,
my foes and my enemies stumble and
fell.
[3] Though an army deploy against me,
my heart is not afraid;
though war break out against me,
still I am confident.
[4] I have asked one thing from the LORD;
it is what I desire:
to dwell in the house of the LORD
all the days of my life,
gazing on the beauty of the LORD
and seeking Him in His temple.
[5] For He will conceal me in His shelter
in the day of adversity;
He will hide me under the cover of His
tent;
He will set me high on a rock.
[6] Then my head will be high
above my enemies around me;
I will offer sacrifices in His tent with
shouts of joy.
[7] LORD, hear my voice when I call;
be gracious to me and answer me.

⁸ In Your behalf my heart says, "Seek
    My face."
LORD, I will seek Your face.
⁹ Do not hide your face from me;
do not turn Your servant away in anger.
You have been my help;
do not leave me or abandon me,
God of my salvation.
¹⁰ Even if my father and mother abandon
    me,
the LORD cares for me.
¹¹ Because of my adversaries,
show me your way, LORD,
and lead me on a level path.
¹² Do not give me over to the will of
    my foes,
for false witnesses rise up against me,
breathing violence.
¹³ I am certain that I will see the LORD's
    goodness
in the land of the living.
Wait for the LORD;
be courageous and let your heart be
    strong.
Wait for the LORD.

thoritatively of an earthly temple not yet built, so also we as Christians anticipate seeing God "as He is" (1 John 3:2), in the fullness of heavenly glory.

In the meantime, we have confidence the shelter He provides for us from adversity will be adequate. Whether we are, as verse 5 indicates, hidden in His tent or isolated on a secure rocky citadel, we will be delivered from any incursions they might make on our spiritual position, freeing us up to sing God's praises all day long.

God's deliverance may not look like we expect. It may not come in as timely a fashion as we would have chosen. Yes, as verses 13-14 indicate, the goodness of God will manifest itself. But we may have to wait for it. And sometimes patience is the hardest lesson to learn. However, a wait, even a protracted one, does not mean God does not see our trials or that He is not helping us in ways we may not appreciate or even recognize. We can be fully confident that if we do our job—remain vigilant, "be courageous and let your heart be strong"—then God will be there when we need Him.

1. From what exactly does God provide salvation? From what does He not promise salvation? Explain. _____
   _____
   _____
   _____

2. If dwelling in the Lord's house is truly our fondest desire, how will that desire manifest itself in day-to-day life on earth? _____
   _____
   _____
   _____

Light and Salt   # Figure of Speech

Perhaps no metaphor is used so frequently and so consistently in the Bible as that of light. Light is used so frequently in reference to God and the things of God that we sometimes cease to even realize it is a figure of speech.

Appropriately, God's first noted interaction with the created universe is to say, "Let there be light" (Genesis 1:3). Ever since then, light has represented God's righteousness (Proverbs 4:18), guidance (Psalm 119:105), and revelation (Luke 2:32). Most of all, it is attached to Jesus Himself, who twice called Himself "the light of the world" (John 8:12, 9:5).

By choosing God's light, we reject Satan's darkness—"He has rescued us from the domain of darkness and transferred us into the kingdom of the Son He loves, in whom we have redemption, the forgiveness of sins" (Colossians 1:13-14). By persisting in the light of Jesus, Christians can avoid "the blackness of darkness forever" (Jude 13) and live forever where "the Lord God will give them light" (Revelation 22:5).

---

3. In what circumstances might we be asked to "wait for the LORD"? _____

_____

_____

_____

4. What is your favorite line in the psalm, and why? _____

_____

_____

_____

The Confident: A Bible Study

"After him, Eleazar son of Dodo son of Ahohi was among the three warriors with David when they defied the Philistines. The men of Israel retreated in the place they had gathered for battle, but Eleazar stood his ground and attacked the Philistines until his hand was tired and stuck to his sword. The LORD brought about a great victory that day. Then the troops came back to him, but only to plunder the dead" (2 Samuel 23:9-10).

This is literally the only mention anywhere in the Bible of Eleazar son of Dodo. Clearly though, as one of the three greatest warriors of David's army, he had quite a reputation among the people and with David himself. No doubt the incident referenced in 2 Samuel 23 is one reason, perhaps the primary reason, he acquired this reputation.

The confidence he shows in his battle with the Philistines is remarkable. He could have retreated (as the rest of the army seems to have done) because the Israelites were, as ever, hopelessly outmatched militarily. He could have retreated at the point of physical exhaustion; he appears to have fought so hard and for so long that his hand was not able to unclench at the end of the conflict. He could have maintained a defensive position and waited until his situation required him to fight instead of taking the battle to the enemy. But Eleazar was not interested in making excuses. He was interested in making war. Because of His courageous stand, God and His people carried the day.

In the same way, we can retreat from spiritual conflict that seems beyond our ability to cope, or quit when we feel that we have "done enough." We can sit back and wait for Satan to come to us instead of actively engaging sin. But the person who derives his confidence from the Lord rather than his own capacity or circumstances will remain confident even in such circumstances.

As a sad epilogue to the story, Eleazar's fellow soldiers returned to the battlefield when the fighting was over "to plunder the dead." They were unwilling to do the work and take the risk, but they were more than ready to claim the fruits of Eleazar's labor. Unfortunately, as confident as we may be that our cause is just and our efforts will be rewarded, we should also be confident that others will try to get by with less and profit more. Instead of becoming resentful or regretful, we should rejoice that God has been glorified, and pray that others find the heart, through our example or others', to serve God more faithfully.

Read Psalm 27 again—this time with Eleazar in mind.

1. What conflicts do we face in our spiritual struggles that would seem to depend on the support we get from other Christians? Do we really need their support?
   _____
   _____
   _____
   _____

2. What ground needs defending in the modern day? How are we doing at defending it? _____
   _____
   _____
   _____

Psalm 121—A Parallel Study

In times of trouble, where do we look? And if it is not toward God, why would it not be? Not only is He "the Maker of heaven and earth" (v.2) and necessarily superior to anything found in either heaven or earth, He has also personally committed Himself to us, His special people. As Israel of old could safely put their confidence in Him, so also may we, the faithful, the true inheritors of Abraham (Galatians 3:6-7).

Of course, Israelites died—even when they were found faithful. When the psalmist says, "The LORD will protect you from all harm; He will protect your life" in verse 7, he is using figurative language. He is not saying God's chosen ones will never suffer; he is saying they are always safe in His care—and particularly, that the eternal life they entrust to Him is secure.

1. Does God's promise to not allow our feet to slip assure us that we cannot fall from grace? Explain. _____
   _____
   _____
   _____

2. Do we need protection from the sun and moon? If not, what does the assurance of verse 6 mean to us? _____
   _____
   _____
   _____

3. How does God protect "your coming and going" (v.8)? _____
   _____
   _____
   _____

4. What is your favorite line in the psalm? Why? _____
   _____
   _____
   _____

The Confident: A Case Study

Enrique was champing at the bit to have a public discussion about the necessity of baptism with a campus evangelist from a denominational group in town. The two of them had struck up an acquaintance at the preacher's discussion table on the

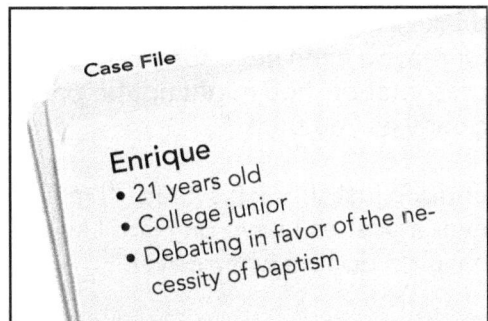

Case File

Enrique
- 21 years old
- College junior
- Debating in favor of the necessity of baptism

campus grounds, and the subject quickly gravitated toward baptism for (or not for) remission of sins.

"He's agreed to give me equal time," Enrique told me, excited. "We'll both make short introductory comments, uninterrupted. Then we will take questions and answers from one another, then questions and answers from the audience."

"Sounds like an interesting afternoon," I told him. "Do you want me to help you with your prep?"

He grinned and shook his head. "I'm not doing any prep. I'm not reading any books or magazines. That's the whole point. I'm going to show up for the discussion with my Bible and that's it. No notes, no nothing."

"Really?"

"It's like with David and Goliath. Showing up with the right tools isn't nearly as important as having God on your side. And if I have truth on my side, I have God, right?"

"Absolutely."

"And I have truth."

"Well, I certainly think so."

"So there you are. I don't need any special arguments or 'Gotcha!' questions. And like you're always saying, baptism for remission of sins is not that difficult an issue for someone with a truly open mind. Just reading the Bible will be enough for anyone who is a true seeker of truth."

"True. But realize, he's going to be using the Bible, too."

"*Mis*-using it, you mean."

"OK, misusing. Still, he's bound to have heard most or all of the points you are going to bring up. He probably has some pat responses ready to go. Don't you think being able to anticipate his next move might be a valuable skill to have? Or maybe even have someone play "devil's advocate" with regard to your own presentation. You might not be presenting your point of view as completely and clearly as you think."

Enrique just shook his head. "I'm not worried about all of that. I'm casting whatever anxieties I have on Him. I know the Scriptures. God will see me through. I have no doubts whatsoever."

Read Psalm 27 again—this time with Enrique in mind.

What would you say to Enrique based on Psalm 27? _____
_____
_____
_____

New Testament Insight

"Lord, I will seek Your face."
Do not hide Your face from me;
do not turn Your servant away in anger.
— Psalm 27:8-9

John 1:18 reads, "No one has ever seen God. The One and Only Son—the One who is at the Father's side—He has revealed Him." No one has seen God because God is spirit (John 4:24). It is not possible for us, as flesh and blood humans, to perceive God in His true nature. That is why we must be transformed to receive our heavenly home (1 Corinthians 15:50).

This tells us that the manifestations of God of which we read in the Old Testament (Genesis 3:8-10; 18:16-22; etc.) were accomplished through the agency of angels, even when the angels are not specifically mentioned. One of the best illustrations of this phenomenon is seen in Exodus 3:18-23, in which Moses requests to see the full glory of God but instead is only shown His back; the "face" of God—i.e., His fullness of Deity—could not be seen, even by Moses.

Jesus changes that. For the first time, mankind was able to stare upon God, as God had for the first time truly taken on flesh (Philippians 2:5-8; Colossians 2:9). Thus by looking at Jesus, His character and His will, we see "fleshed out" the person of God Almighty. "For God, who said, 'Light shall shine out of darkness'—He has shone in our hearts to give the light of the knowledge of God's glory in the face of Jesus Christ" (2 Corinthians 4:6).

The Confident: A Hymn Study

Other than adaptations of actual Biblical texts, "Be Thou My Vision" may be the oldest hymn extant, dating back almost a millennium and a half.

The man who came to be known as Saint Patrick was born in 373 A.D. near the River Clyde in what is now Scotland. He was kidnapped by pirates and taken to Ireland at the age of 16. But he escaped, learned about Jesus, and eventually returned to his captors to teach them.

Be Thou My Vision

1. Be Thou my vi - sion, O Lord of my heart;
2. Be Thou my wis - dom and Thou my true word;
3. Rich - es I heed not, nor man's emp - ty praise,
4. High King of heav - en, my vic - to - ry won,

Naught be all else to me, save that Thou art.
I ev - er with Thee and Thou with me, Lord;
Thou my in - her - it - ance, now and al - ways:
May I reach heav - en's joys, O bright heav'n's Sun!

Thou my best thought, by day or by night,
Thou my great Fa - ther, I Thy true son;
Thou and Thou on - ly, first in my heart,
Heart of my heart, what - ev - er be - fall,

Wak - ing or sleep - ing, Thy pres - ence my light.
Thou in me dwell - ing, and I with Thee one.
High King of heav - en, my treas - ure Thou art.
Still be my vi - sion, O Rul - er of all.

Words: Irish Folk Hymn, tr. Mary E. Byrne, alt. Eleanor H.Hull
Music: Joyce's *Old Irish Folk Music and Songs*, arr. C. E. Couchman
Arr. © 2009 C. E. Couchman

E - 3 - DO

The story goes that around the year 433, Patrick defied the edict of King Logaire of Tara that prohibited the lighting of candles on the eve of Easter Sunday; a pagan festival was to feature a bonfire on Slane Hill, and no fires were to be lit that would take away from it. The king was so impressed by Patrick's zeal that he allowed him to continue his work spreading God's word. Tradition credits him for establishing 2,000 churches throughout Ireland, teaching more than 100,000 natives.

A 6th Century monk named Dallan Forgaill is generally thought to have written the words to "Be Thou My Vision" in tribute to Saint Patrick's commitment against great opposition. Mary E. Byrne translated the verses from Irish into English in 1905, and an old Irish tune called "Slade" was adapted to fit the hymn.

With the modern upturn in interest in traditional Irish music, "Be Thou My Vision" has achieved a new popularity. It has been recorded in recent years by numerous religious music groups and by pop musician Van Morrison. It was named one of the 15 most popular hymns in the United Kingdom by the BBC's "Songs of Praise" in 2013.

The Confident: A Worship Study

"Did you know 'Be Thou My Vision' was written by a blind man?" asked Edward, one of our senior citizens who himself had almost completely lost his sight.

"I didn't know that," I admitted.

"That's the story, anyway. Dallan Forgaill, or 'Saint Dallan,' back in the 6th Century. The story goes that he was blind. Interesting, considering the song."

"Is that why you love it so much?" Edward could not read out of our hymnals, but he sang well from memory. However, "Be Thou My Vision" was not one of the church's standards.

"Oh no, I've loved that song for years. But I'll confess to developing a bit of … shall we say, ironic pleasure in the lyric in recent years. As you know, I'm not passing many eye tests these days. And I suspect that trend isn't going to change. But I see the things I need to see just fine."

"What do you mean by that?" I asked, largely for the others who had gathered to hear Edward talk, as I had heard him discuss the topic numerous times.

"I mean, I've never seen the really important things. Heaven. Judgment. Jesus Himself. I've always let God do my seeing for me. You know, 2 Corinthians 5:7."

"For we walk by faith, not by sight," we all recite as one.

"Exactly," Edward continued. "So now, as it is becoming increasingly impossible to see anything else, I am finding it easier and easier as the end draws closer to look only at those things. And I find them coming into sharper and sharper focus. And that's a good thing."

What does "Be Thou My Vision" mean to you? _____

_____

_____

_____

The Bible Study Song List

If you were putting a list together for a study about confidence, what songs would you include? Why? _____

_____

_____

What songs might you exclude? Why? _____

_____

_____

_____

www.ingramcontent.com/pod-product-compliance
Lightning Source LLC
LaVergne TN
LVHW061327060426
835511LV00012B/1907